Painless Project Management with FogBugz

MIKE GUNDERLOY

Painless Project Management with FogBugz

Copyright © 2005 by Mike Gunderloy

ISBN (pbk): 1-59059-486-X

Printed and bound in the United States of America 9 8 7 6 5 4 3 2 1

Lead Editor: Gary Cornell
Technical Reviewer: Joel Spolsky
Editorial Board: Steve Anglin, Dan Appleman, Ewan Buckingham, Gary Cornell, Tony Davis, Jason Gilmore, Jonathan Hassell, Chris Mills, Dominic Shakeshaft, Jim Sumser
Project Manager: Beth Christmas
Copy Edit Manager: Nicole LeClerc
Copy Editor: Ami Knox
Production Manager: Kari Brooks-Copony
Production Editor: Katie Stence
Compositor: Susan Glinert
Proofreader: Ellie Fountain
Indexer: Michael Brinkman
Artist: Kinetic Publishing Services, LLC
Cover Designer: Kurt Krames
Manufacturing Manager: Tom Debolski

Distributed to the book trade in the United States by Springer-Verlag New York, Inc., 233 Spring Street, 6th Floor, New York, NY 10013, and outside the United States by Springer-Verlag GmbH & Co. KG, Tiergartenstr. 17, 69112 Heidelberg, Germany.

In the United States: phone 1-800-SPRINGER, fax 201-348-4505, e-mail orders@springer-ny.com, or visit http://www.springer-ny.com. Outside the United States: fax +49 6221 345229, e-mail orders@springer.de, or visit http://www.springer.de.

For information on translations, please contact Apress directly at 2560 Ninth Street, Suite 219, Berkeley, CA 94710. Phone 510-549-5930, fax 510-549-5939, e-mail info@apress.com, or visit http://www.apress.com.

For all the ladies at PS I Love You, who watched me write and edit this book.

Contents at a Glance

Contents

Foreword

There's a restaurant in my New York City neighborhood called Isabella's that's always packed.

Downstairs, upstairs, at the sidewalk cafe, it's mobbed. And there are large crowds of happy yuppies out front, waiting 45 minutes for a table when they can *clearly* see other *perfectly good* restaurants right across the street that have plenty of tables.

It doesn't matter when you go there. For Sunday brunch, it's packed. Friday night? Packed, of course. But go on a quiet Wednesday night at 11:00 p.m. You'll get a table fairly quickly, but the restaurant is still, basically, packed.

Is it the food? Nah. Ruth Reichl, restaurant reviewer extraordinaire from the *New York Times*, dismissed it thusly: "The food is not very good."[1]

The prices? I doubt anyone cares. This is the neighborhood where Jerry Seinfeld bought Isaac Stern's apartment with views over *two* parks.

Lack of competition? What, are you serious? This is Manhattan!

Here's a clue as to why Isabella's works. In ten years living in this neighborhood, I still go back there. All the time. Because they've never given me a single reason not to.

That actually says a lot.

I never go to a certain fake-Italian art-themed restaurant, because once I ate there and the waiter, who had gone beyond rude well into the realm of actual cruelty, mocking our entree choices, literally chased us down the street complaining about the small tip we left him.

I stopped going to another hole-in-the-wall pizza-pasta-bistro because the owner would come sit down at our table while we ate and ask for computer help.

I really, really loved the food at a local curry restaurant with headache-inducing red banquettes and zebra-striped decor. The katori chat was *to die for*. I was even willing to overlook the noxious smell of ammonia wafting up from the subterranean bathrooms. But the food inevitably took an hour to arrive, even when the place was empty, so I just never went back.

But in ten years, I can't think of a single bad thing that ever happened to me at Isabella's. Nothing.

So that's why it's so packed. People keep coming back, again and again, because when you dine at Isabella's, nothing will ever go wrong.

Isabella's is thoroughly and completely debugged.

It takes you ten years to notice this, because most of the time when you eat at a restaurant, nothing goes wrong. It took a couple of years of going to the curry place before we realized they were always going to make us miss our movie, no matter how early we arrived, and we finally had to write them off.

And so, on the Upper West Side of Manhattan, if you're a restaurant, and you want to thrive, you have to carefully debug everything.

---

1. Reichl, Ruth. The New York Times ➤ Travel ➤ New York City Guide ➤ Restaurant Details ("Isabella's Restaurant") (Web page). http://travel2.nytimes.com/top/features/travel/destinations/unitedstates/newyork/newyorkcity/restaurant_details.html?vid=1002207988079, dated 4/98, retrieved December 9, 2005.

You have to make sure that there's always someone waiting to greet guests. This person must learn never to leave the maitre d' desk to show someone to their table, because otherwise the next person will come in and there will be nobody there to greet them. Instead, someone else needs to show patrons to their tables. And give them their menus, right away. And take their coats and drink orders.

You have to figure out who your best customers are—the locals who come on weekday nights when the restaurant is relatively quiet—and give them tables quickly on Friday night, even if the out-of-towners have to wait a little longer.

You need a procedure so that every water glass is always full.

Every time somebody is unhappy, that's a bug. Write it down. Figure out what you're going to do about it. Add it to the training manual. Never make the same mistake twice.

Eventually, Isabella's became a fabulously profitable and successful restaurant, not because of its food, but because it was *debugged*. Just getting what we programmers call "the edge cases" right was sufficient to keep people coming back, and telling their friends, and that's enough to overcome a review where the *New York Times* calls your food "not very good."

Great products are great because they're *deeply debugged*. Restaurants, software, it's all the same.

Great software doesn't crash when you do weird, rare things, because everybody does something weird.

Microsoft developer Larry Osterman, working on DOS 4, once thought he had found a rare bug. "But if that were the case," he told DOS architect Gordon Letwin, "it'd take a one in a million chance for it to happen."

Letwin's reply? "In our business, one in a million is next Tuesday."[2]

Great software helps you out when you misunderstand it. If you try to drag a file to a button in the taskbar, Windows pops up a message that says, essentially, "You can't do that!" but then it goes on to tell you how you can accomplish what you're obviously trying to do. (Try it!)

Great software pops up messages that show that the designers have thought about the problem you're working on, probably more than you have. In FogBugz, for example, if you try to reply to an e-mail message, but someone else tries to reply to that same e-mail at the same time, you get a warning and your response is not sent until you can check out what's going on.

Great software works the way *everybody* expects it to. I'm probably one of the few people left who still closes windows by double-clicking in the top-left corner instead of clicking the X button. I don't know why I do that, but it always works, with great software. Some software that I have is not so great. It doesn't close if you double-click in the top-left corner. That makes me a little bit frustrated. It probably made a lot of people frustrated, and a lot of those people probably complained, but I'll bet you that the software developers just didn't do bug tracking, because they have never fixed that bug and probably never will.

What great software has in common is being *deeply debugged*, and the only way to get software that's deeply debugged is to *keep track of your bugs*.

A bug-tracking database is not just a memory aid or a scheduling tool. It doesn't make it *easier* to produce great software, it makes it *possible* to create great software.

---

2. Osterman, Larry. "One in a million is next Tuesday," from Larry Osterman's WebLog (personal web page). http://blogs.msdn.com/larryosterman/archive/2004/03/30/104165.aspx, dated March 30, 2004, retrieved December 9, 2004.

With bug tracking, every idea gets into the system. Every flaw gets into the system. Every tester's possible misinterpretation of the user interface gets into the system. Every possible improvement that anybody thinks about gets into the system.

Bug-tracking software captures the cosmic rays that cause the genetic mutations that make your software evolve into something superior.

And as you constantly evaluate, reprioritize, triage, punt, and assign these flaws, the software evolves. It gets better and better. It learns to deal with more and more weird situations, more and more misunderstanding users, and more and more scenarios.

That's when something magical happens, and your software becomes better than just the sum of its features. Suddenly it becomes *reliable*. Reliable, meaning, it never screws up. It never makes its users angry. It never makes its customers wish they had purchased something else.

And that magic is the key to success. In restaurants as in software.

—Joel Spolsky

About the Author

MIKE GUNDERLOY has been involved with the computer industry for over a quarter century. In that time, he's assembled PCs, run network cable through drop ceilings, contributed to and managed software projects large and small, as well as written many books and articles. When he's not banging out code or words on the keyboard, Mike raises children, turkeys, and tomatoes on a small farm in eastern Washington state.

About the Technical Reviewer

JOEL SPOLSKY is an expert on software development and the founder of Fog Creek Software. His Web site, Joel on Software (http://www.joelonsoftware.com), is popular with software developers around the world and has been translated into over 30 languages. His latest book is *Joel on Software* (Apress, 2004).

Acknowledgments

Every book starts somewhere. In the case of the current volume, the starting point is easy to pinpoint: an e-mail from Fog Creek Software's Joel Spolsky, asking me if I'd be interested in putting together a book about FogBugz 4.0. After I leapt at (I mean, after I carefully considered and accepted) this proposal, Gary Cornell at Apress was instrumental in pulling together the contractual details necessary to make this book a reality.

Of course, a book about software can't be written without the software itself, and in this case it's easy to know who to thank for that: Joel and the rest of the Fog Creek staff. Special thanks to Michael Pryor, who spent a few maddening hours logged in to one of my computers remotely trying to figure out what I was doing to provoke a particularly obscure bug. Beyond that, the active FogBugz user community is to thank for many of the innovations in this version of FogBugz.

I'd like to thank Project Manager Beth Christmas, Copy Editor Ami Knox, and Production Editor Katie Stence for their hard work turning my manuscript into something actually resembling a book. And let's not forget the hard-working production crew: Compositor Susan Glinert, Proofreader Ellie Fountain, and Indexer Michael Brinkman.

Then there are the people outside of the actual book production process who still deserve huge thanks: my family. With this book, that's even more true than usual, as they were quite understanding about my tackling a new project with an intense schedule during the holiday season. Somehow I managed to take breaks to carve turkey and bake cookies, but it was a near thing. So thanks and much love to my dear wife, Dana, and our kids, Adam, Kayla, and Thomas. Next year I'll take more than a day off, honest.

Introduction

Like any other developer who wants to actually ship software, I use software management tools. One of the most important tools in my own toolbox is FogBugz. Now on its fourth major release, FogBugz is a complete project management system optimized for software teams. It's Web-based, so you access most of the functionality through your Web browser. I've found this an immense help when working with developers and testers scattered about the Internet, but you can also use FogBugz for projects that are maintained entirely at a single location. In this book, you'll see why I'm so excited about FogBugz, and learn what it can do for your own software management tasks.

Why FogBugz?

Many of the software applications that overlap the functionality of FogBugz present themselves as bug-tracking systems, but there's more to FogBugz than just tracking bugs. FogBugz is a tool for tracking, updating, and managing cases. There are three kinds of cases:

- *Bugs*: Things that don't work right

- *Features*: New things being planned

- *Inquiries*: Questions from customers or team members

Every case is prioritized, categorized, and assigned to exactly one person on your team who must either resolve it or assign it to someone else. Developers work through their cases one by one, ideally in order of priority. That doesn't sound like much to handle, but FogBugz integrates case tracking with many other features, including the following:

- Source code control integration, which makes it easy to see which check-ins are associated with which bugs or features, and allows you to set up an elegant online code review system.

- Filters and advanced full-text search that make it easy to sort and search.

- A built-in estimation system to help you track your project and ship on schedule.

- Automatic release note generation from the cases that were resolved for a particular release.

- A customer e-mail management facility that discards spam and sorts the mail into categories based on your own training. FogBugz preserves the entire e-mail history and makes it easy to keep the customer informed of progress on a case.

- Integrated discussion groups for customers, testers, or team members. Discussion groups include anti-spam features and easy integration with case tracking.

What's in This Book

My goal in this book is to take you from the very basics of FogBugz through all the details of managing and administering a complex FogBugz installation. Depending on your role—developer, tester, manager, system administrator, or (as with many of us) jack-of-all-trades—you may want to read some portions of the book more closely than others. Here's a roadmap of what you'll find inside:

In Chapter 1, you'll learn about the overall philosophy of FogBugz (yes, software applications have philosophies) and get an introduction to how FogBugz works in practice. I'll take you through the lifecycle of several cases so that you can get a feel for how the pieces fit together.

Chapter 2 concentrates on the actual process of case management with FogBugz. You'll learn how cases get into the system and how to deal with them once they've been entered. This chapter covers taking screenshots and attaching files, as well as filtering and sorting to find the cases that you need.

Chapter 3 is directed mainly at the FogBugz administrator. While many organizations will be able to use FogBugz productively right out of the box, there are quite a few pieces of the program that you can customize. If you're the one responsible for fine-tuning FogBugz where you work, this is the chapter for you. You'll learn how to set up projects, areas, clients, departments, and much more.

Chapter 4 looks at FogBugz from the perspective of the software manager. This is the chapter that covers estimating techniques, due dates, the proper way to resolve cases, and release notes. I'll also dip a little bit into using external tools such as Microsoft Access and Microsoft Excel to create custom reports from your FogBugz data.

Chapter 5 covers customer communication via e-mail and discussion groups. Some of the most innovative and exciting features of version 4.0 are in this area, and you'll want to read this chapter closely. These features let you connect your FogBugz database directly with your customers, tapping their collective intelligence and excitement.

Finally, in Chapter 6, I cover the integration of FogBugz with your source code control system. You'll learn why you might want to do this, and how to set it up if you're using CVS, Perforce, Subversion, Vault, or Visual SourceSafe.

The book wraps up with two appendixes. Appendix A reviews the instructions for installing FogBugz on Windows, Linux, or Mac OS X servers. Appendix B shows how you can write code to integrate your own applications directly with FogBugz for automatic bug reporting.

I hope that by the end of the book you'll consider yourself a serious FogBugz user, and that you'll find this program as useful and well designed as I do.

Contacting the Author

I'm always happy to hear from readers of any of my books. You can find my own Web site at http://www.larkware.com, or e-mail me directly at MikeG1@larkfarm.com. But in the case of FogBugz questions, there's another resource you should try for a quick response: the FogBugz discussion group at http://support.fogcreek.com/?fogbugz. You'll find many passionate and committed FogBugz users there who are happy to help out, as well as Fog Creek's own support staff.

■ ■ ■

CHAPTER 1

Managing Projects with FogBugz

Communication is the lifeblood of a software project. Whether you're building an application for commercial sale or developing it for internal corporate use, there's no way that a software project can be successful without customer feedback. Communication within the team that's building the application is equally important. Developers, testers, and managers all need to coordinate their activities with each other to make sure the product gets out the door on time and with the right features.

Software teams manage this communication with a variety of tools and technologies: whiteboards, e-mails, phone calls, sticky notes, hallway meetings, formal review sessions, and more. But there's a danger to using too many tools to manage a software project: the more places you have to store information and the more ways you have to pass it around, the easier it is for important messages to fall through the cracks. In this book, I'll show you how to use one tool—Fog Creek Software's FogBugz 4.0—to collect and manage all of the communication between users, managers, developers, and testers. With FogBugz in place, you'll spend less time hunting for information and trying to remember who was doing what, and have more time to finish the product on time and within budget.

FogBugz from the Mountain Top

As you work through this book, you'll learn all the nitty-gritty details of working with FogBugz. But before setting out on this journey, it's good to know where you're going. FogBugz came from some simple notions of what a bug-tracking tool should do. From those roots, though, it's grown into a robust project management tool. You may also need some other tools (for example, something to graphically display the project schedule and dependencies), but FogBugz can form the core of a successful project management strategy for most software projects.

Note The early versions of FogBugz did indeed concentrate on tracking bugs—hence the name of the product. But the more robust capabilities of FogBugz 4.0 move it beyond the bug-tracking category to make it more of a project-tracking tool. It's too late to rename the product, though.

Understanding the FogBugz Philosophy

FogBugz is based on two core principles:

- Track as much product-related communication as possible in a single tool.

- Keep everything as simple as possible (but no simpler!).

By sticking to these principles, Fog Creek has been able to deliver a tool that can be installed in minutes and that the average developer can start using immediately. Unlike some products in the field, FogBugz does not let you customize everything. Excessive flexibility can lead to an organizational paralysis while people debate which bug statuses to use, how to organize work-flow, and so on. In contrast, FogBugz lets you customize the things that really vary between organizations (like the name of the project that you're working on), while delivering a robust set of core features that just work.

Note For more information on installing FogBugz, see Appendix A.

Surveying FogBugz

FogBugz is a client-server system with a Web client. The information that you store in FogBugz is tracked in a database and presented through a series of scripted pages on a Web server (depending on your choice of platform, the scripting language is either ASP or PHP). To the users, this means a FogBugz installation looks like any other Web site. You can interact with FogBugz through any modern Web browser, including Internet Explorer, Mozilla, Firefox, or Opera. You can even use a mobile device such as a PocketPC or a SmartPhone to work with FogBugz (though you may find using the small screen challenging).

The features of FogBugz break up into three categories:

- Case tracking

- E-mail management

- Discussion group management

I'll briefly discuss each of these areas in turn.

Case Tracking

Cases are the key unit in the database that FogBugz maintains. Each case is assigned to one of three categories:

- *Features*: New functionality to be added to the product

- *Bugs*: Existing functionality that doesn't work right

- *Inquiries*: Questions from customers or other stakeholders

Figure 1-1 shows a typical case (it happens to be a bug) in FogBugz. As you can see, each case is characterized by a variety of properties, including its priority, the release that needs to include the fix, and the history of work on the case.

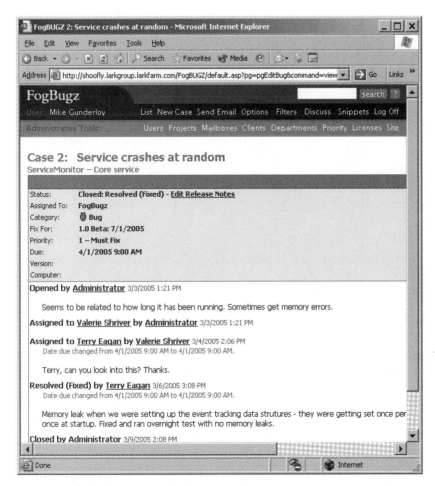

Figure 1-1. *A typical case in FogBugz*

Cases can be entered manually by any licensed user of FogBugz. They can also be created in several other ways. For example, cases can be automatically created from e-mail received at a specific address, created by a site administrator based on a discussion group thread, or even automatically added to the database by special code in an application that you've already shipped.

FogBugz lets users filter cases to find only the set they're interested in at the moment (for example, all open cases assigned to you that are due for the next release). You can use the FogBugz Web interface to adjust the properties of a case or assign an estimate to it. When you're done fixing a bug, implementing a feature, or handling an inquiry, you can mark it resolved. This automatically assigns the case back to its originator, who can close it (thus removing it from the list of active cases).

■**Tip** Only the originator of a case can close it. If you can't convince the person who spotted a bug that it's fixed, then it's not fixed.

FogBugz also offers other features related to case management. If you're interested in a particular case, you can subscribe to it so as to receive e-mail notification whenever the case is changed. You can also subscribe to RSS feeds that provide an overall view of case activity. FogBugz integrates with a number of popular source code control systems so that you can track which code fixes are related to which bugs. You can even create a set of release notes automatically from the cases that were fixed for a particular release.

■**Note** You'll learn more about managing FogBugz cases in Chapter 2.

E-Mail Management

FogBugz also helps you manage incoming product-related e-mail from your customers. This isn't a substitute for your existing e-mail server, but a way to handle e-mail sent to specific addresses. For example, you might use CustServ@megautil.com as a general customer service e-mail address, and ServMonBugs@megautil.com as an address to accept bug reports on your Service Monitor application.

You can set up FogBugz to monitor any number of POP3 mailboxes for incoming mail. When mail arrives, FogBugz applies a series of steps to sort it appropriately. First, spam is automatically discarded. For other messages, you have a choice of manual sorting or autosorting. If you choose to manually sort messages, FogBugz will create a new case in the project of your choice for each incoming message. Autosort is much more sophisticated. You can create a set of categories, and autosort will learn by example which messages belong in which category. With autosort, you start by moving messages manually, but FogBugz soon takes over the job, creating new cases in categories just as you would have done yourself.

Customers who send e-mail to a properly configured FogBugz POP3 address will get an automatic reply return, with a URL where they can check the progress of their case in the system. Any member of the development team can respond to e-mail messages and see the whole history of communications with the user when doing so. The system can automatically assign a due date to make sure that customers get replies in a timely fashion. To make it easier to generate those replies, you can also create predefined text snippets that can be inserted into a return e-mail with just a few keystrokes.

Discussion Group Management

E-mail is good for one-on-one communication, but there are times when a conversation benefits from wider input. For example, you might have a group of developers and testers who want to discuss how a particular feature should work, or a group of customers with feedback and suggestions for future versions of the application. To handle this sort of many-to-many communication, FogBugz includes support for online discussion groups.

FogBugz discussion groups are simple. You can set up any number of groups on your server and give them each a distinct name. Each group contains threads, and each thread contains messages. Messages are presented as a chronologically ordered list, without any branching; this makes it easy to catch up with any conversation by starting wherever you left off.

The discussion group implementation includes anti-spam technology to prevent junk from cluttering up the real discussion, and moderation to help weed out disruptive messages or unruly users. You can customize the appearance of a discussion group so that it fits in with your corporate Web site. A single button click will turn a discussion group message into a case, so that problems and suggestions reported via discussion group don't get lost.

Getting Down to Business

To get a better understanding for how FogBugz can help with your development cycle, let's follow a couple of typical cases from start to finish.

For these examples, I'll introduce MegaUtilities Corporation, a fictional company that writes and (with any luck) sells software utilities for the Microsoft Windows market. Their products include Network Enumerator (a general-purpose network browser), ScriptGen (an automated generator for command scripts), and Service Monitor (a Windows service that monitors the event log and sends e-mail when it recognizes a particular message). MegaUtilities has a comparatively small staff: two administrators, a single project manager, a customer service representative, four developers, and three testers.

Moving a Bug Through the System

During the beta period for Service Monitor, Robert Evers (who is the company's customer service rep) logs on to FogBugz and, as part of his daily duties, reviews the new postings to the Service Monitor discussion group. He finds the new thread shown in Figure 1-2 (fortunately, there are lots of other threads from happy customers, so the beta isn't a complete disaster).

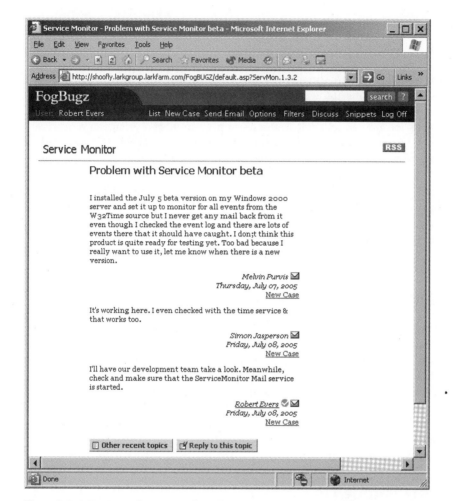

Figure 1-2. *A FogBugz discussion thread*

MegaUtilities has the sensible policy of never ignoring customer complaints, no matter how outlandish or ungrammatical they are. Even though another customer has already replied to the first poster, Robert uses the New Case hyperlink (which only appears because he's logged in as a user on the server) to create a new FogBugz case to track this particular bug. FogBugz automatically grabs the title and description from the discussion group posting, so all Robert has to do is fill in other information and click OK to create the case.

■**Tip** This example shows in a small way one of the benefits of discussion groups: other customers will do some of your support for you. The more effort you expend in building a broad base of users on your discussion groups, the more chance there is that frequent posters will emerge and answer questions before your own paid staff can even read them.

Robert chooses the Service Monitor project, and FogBugz automatically assigns the bug to the project lead. Because this particular bug is a direct failure of the core functionality of the product, he marks it as a priority 1 bug for the 1.0 release version of the product. Robert then returns to the discussion group thread, clicks the Reply To This Topic button, and types a reply to let the original poster know that his problem is being looked at.

Meanwhile, FogBugz itself has not been idle. As soon as the new case gets created and assigned to the project lead, Valerie Shriver, FogBugz sends her e-mail to tell her that there's something new on her plate. Because Valerie is a Type A personality who always keeps her e-mail running, she gets this notification in short order. Clicking the link in the e-mail takes her directly to the case. Although she doubts that even a beta could get out the door if it wasn't working at all (and she knows that it's happily monitoring events in the company lab in any case), Valerie also knows that she can't just ignore a prospective customer. Fortunately, she has development staff to take care of these things for her. So she clicks the Assign button, assigns the bug to Paige Nagel, and adds a comment guessing at the cause of the bug.

■**Tip** When you want to assign a case to another user, choose the Assign button rather than the Edit button. While either one will move the case over, only the Assign button will automatically send an e-mail notification as well.

Of course, FogBugz e-mails Paige to tell her the bug is on her plate now. Paige doesn't see how this bug can be happening either, but she dutifully sets up Service Monitor on one of the lab machines and tells it to monitor for W32Time events. She deliberately assigns a bogus time server to the machine so that events will end up in the event log. Sure enough, she gets the notification e-mails just as she should. Paige has other things to do, and this one really looks like pilot error to her, so she clicks the Resolve button. She chooses "Resolved (Not Reproducible)" as the status and saves her changes.

But remember, resolving a bug doesn't get rid of it. Instead, it goes back to Robert, who was the one who entered the case into the system in the first place. Robert feels strongly about protecting his customers, and he's not going to take "not reproducible" as a resolution without a fight. He thinks about some of the issues they saw when alpha testing, looks at the customer's e-mail address, and comes to his own conclusion about the possible cause of the bug. So he reactivates the bug, adds a comment, and shoots it back over to Paige.

This time Paige grumbles a bit about the added effort to set up a good repro case (after all, she has new features to implement, not just bugs to fix!), but she gets to work. A few minutes later she has a test Hotmail account of her own, and a few minutes after that, she verifies that she can reproduce the problem. This puts her 90% of the way to fixing it. She changes the format of the message so that it looks less "spammy" and marks the bug as "Resolved (Fixed)." This bounces it back to Robert again.

Robert uses the private e-mail feature of the discussion group to send a message to the original poster, asking him to check his Hotmail spam folder for the missing messages. Sure enough, there they are, and Robert logs back into FogBugz to close the case. Figure 1-3 shows the final state of the closed case. As you can see, it preserves the entire history and lets you see just what happened, beginning with the original report.

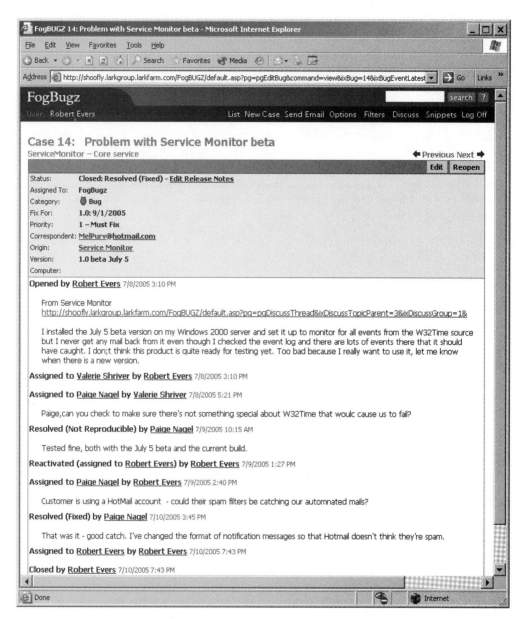

Figure 1-3. *A closed case in FogBugz*

Responding to a Customer Inquiry

My second example highlights the e-mail management features of FogBugz. This time I'll
follow what happens when a customer inquiry arrives by e-mail. Simon Jasperson, who happens
to be a long-time user of MegaUtilities products, had planned to be an enthusiastic tester of
Service Monitor. But when he tried to install the product, the installation failed. From reading
the release notes with the beta, he knows that he can send e-mail to CustServ@megautil.com
describing his problem, so he does so.

Back at MegaUtilities, Randy Wilson happens to be logged on to the FogBugz server when he notices a new case in the Inbox project. Any FogBugz user can review and deal with incoming mail, so Randy clicks through to the message. It looks like a legitimate bug to him, so he moves it over to the Service Monitor project and lets FogBugz assign it to the primary contact, Valerie Shriver.

Meanwhile, FogBugz doesn't forget about the customer. Simon gets back an automatically generated e-mail that not only tells him his message has been received, but gives him a URL for tracking what's going on with it. Clicking through to the URL gives him a read-only view of the case, as shown in Figure 1-4.

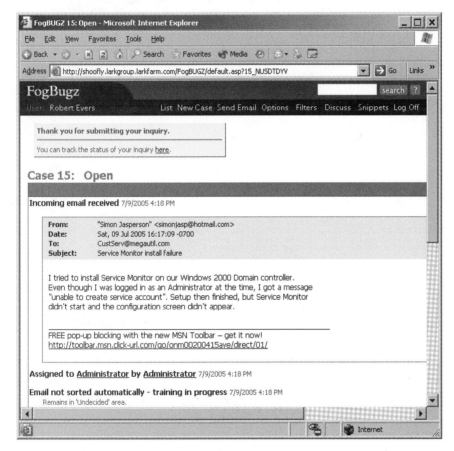

Figure 1-4. *Customer view of an open case*

The bug proceeds through the usual process at MegaUtilities. Valerie adds a due date to the bug and assigns it over to Terry Eagan, another of her developers. Terry is pretty swamped right now, but she opens the bug and puts in an initial estimate of 6 hours to solve the problem. All of these changes continue to be reflected on the status page that Simon can check out, assuring him that the company is working on his problem.

In a few days, Terry has time to track down the actual problem, and fixes the code so that it works—at least on her test machine. She marks the bug as fixed, and FogBugz assigns it to the

FogBugz administrator (because it can't be assigned to a customer). The administrator later signs on to look at the bug on behalf of the customer. Seeing that the bug is fixed, she clicks the Reply button in the bug's header, which automatically composes an e-mail back to the customer, as shown in Figure 1-5. The administrator uses this e-mail to close the loop back to the original customer, letting him know that the bug is fixed in the latest build, and then closes the bug.

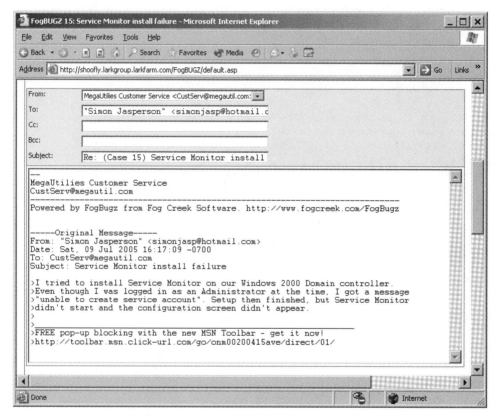

Figure 1-5. *Sending e-mail back to a customer*

Making Effective Use of FogBugz

FogBugz is a great program, but it isn't miraculous. No amount of management technology will make your software projects successful all by itself. FogBugz can help by making it easy to track and resolve issues, and by making sure that communication with the all-important customer doesn't get ignored. But you also need to do some work on the social level, to make sure that FogBugz gets used, and used well.

Bringing FogBugz into Your Company

The first hurdle to using FogBugz is to get it used at all. Here, the first few cases may be the hardest. After people see how easy FogBugz is to use, and how much it helps them work, they'll probably start using it on their own. So how do you jump-start the process?

If you sign the paychecks, you can just tell everyone to use the new bug-tracking system. But this may not be the most effective option. Telling programmers what to do has frequently been referred to as "herding cats," and it is just about as effective. Instead, start using FogBugz yourself. Put in some bugs or feature requests (if you don't know enough about your own company's products to make sensible feature requests, why are you in charge?). Then you can suggest to people that they'd better keep an eye on the system if they don't want to lose your valuable input. This will usually get through.

If you're a manager, and nobody seems to be using FogBugz, start assigning new features to your team using FogBugz. Eventually they'll realize that instead of coming into your office every few days saying "What should I do next?" they can just see what's assigned to them in FogBugz. If you're using an agile process where new features get assigned during a consensual meeting, have someone enter the features into FogBugz right there at the meeting.

If you're a developer, and you're having trouble getting testers to use FogBugz, just don't accept bug reports by any other method. If your testers are used to sending you e-mail with bug reports, just bounce the e-mails back to them with a brief message: "Please put this in the bug database. I can't keep track of e-mail." If you're a developer, and only some of your colleagues use FogBugz, just start assigning them bugs. Eventually they'll get the hint.

If you're a tester, and you're having trouble getting programmers to use FogBugz, just don't tell them about bugs—put them in the database and let the database e-mail them. This can be especially effective if you can also convince the manager for the project to subscribe to the RSS feed for the bugs. Most developers have at least enough political savvy to want to stay as informed as their boss.

Writing Good Bug Reports

It's not enough to get everyone in the company using FogBugz. You also need to get them using it *well*. The key here is to teach people to write good bug reports. For starters, every bug report should contain the three essential pieces of information:

- How to make the bug happen

- What happened

- What should have happened

Put that way, it looks easy, right? But if you've ever spent time trying to actually respond to bug reports, you know that writing good bug reports is harder than it looks. People post all sorts of crazy things to bug databases (and that's not even counting spam, which FogBugz fortunately does a good job of weeding out before it gets to you).

When you think you've found a bug, the first step is to record the information about how to reproduce the bug. The key problem here is to include just the necessary information. Determining what's necessary is an art. What you had for breakfast this morning probably doesn't have a bearing on the bug (unless you're testing dietary analysis software). The operating system on your computer and the amount of RAM could have a bearing. The last action you took in the application almost certainly does make a difference.

Whatever information you can collect, please organize it sensibly. Programmers tend to be focused on careful instructions, so step-by-step details are very useful. Figure 1-6 shows a bug with a good set of reproduction steps.

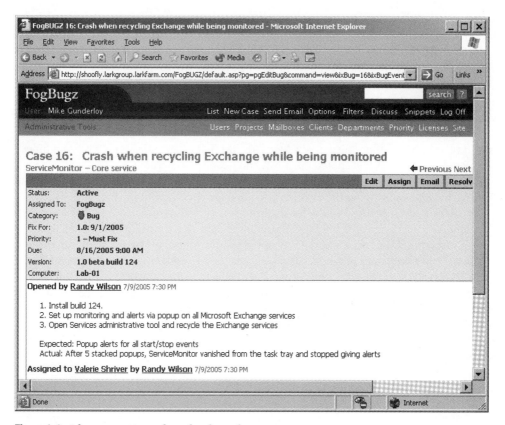

Figure 1-6. *A bug report to make a developer happy*

Sometimes it's just not possible to come up with good repro steps. Perhaps you used the application for quite a while and it suddenly crashed, and you don't remember what you were doing. In that case, write down everything you remember. Perhaps you thought you had the steps, but they don't always make the bug happen. In that case, record the steps, but please also tell the developer that the bug is intermittent. Otherwise, it'll probably just get closed as not reproducible.

The second piece of information you need to supply is what happened that made you think this was a bug. Did the program destroy all the files on your hard drive? Did Windows expire in the fabled Blue Screen of Death? Did the developers just spell a word wrong on-screen? This information often makes the best title for the bug as well; something like "Shift-Enter fills hard drive with temporary files" is easy to recognize when you're just scanning down a list of titles.

Finally, tell the developer what should have happened instead. "Sausauge should be spelled sausage" will help guide the poor developer who wasn't at the top of his English class. At times you can omit this piece of information because it will be implied by the description of what happened. If you report it as a bug that the program failed to install on a particular operating system, it's a safe bet that you expected it to install. But when in doubt, be explicit.

Writing Good Feature Requests

Feature requests, too, require careful composition. When you enter a feature request into the FogBugz database, you're saying one of two things:

- "This feature is part of the spec, and now it's your job."

- "I know no one thought of this earlier, but I think it's really, really important."

Any project that requires enough work to justify using FogBugz at all should have a formal, written specification. Specs are enormously important, because they represent the shared vision of how the product should work when it's finished. Developers refer to the spec to figure out how all the pieces fit together, testers use it to figure out what to test (and to see whether a particular piece of behavior is a bug or a feature), managers use it to help schedule to project, and so on. The product's spec should be a collective, comprehensive, up-to-date vision of the way that the product will work.

■**Note** For more detail on writing good functional specifications, see Joel Spolsky's book *Joel on Software* (Apress, 2004).

But although the spec is important, it doesn't quite get you all the way to working code. Someone has to take all of those features in the spec and assign them to individual developers to implement. Now, you (assuming you're the program manager) could do that with e-mail or notes on a whiteboard or orders shouted down the hall, but with FogBugz installed, you've got a better solution: enter them as feature requests in FogBugz. You can cut and paste the appropriate part of the spec into the feature request, and include a hyperlink to the full spec on your network (you *do* have the spec stored on a server where everyone can read it, right?).

An added benefit of using FogBugz to assign features is that it will help you schedule the entire project. If your developers use the estimating features of FogBugz, you can look at the total amount of work left to be done, and adjust your schedule (or your feature set) as necessary.

■**Note** For more information on estimating in FogBugz, see Chapter 4.

The other use for feature requests in FogBugz is to handle features that you didn't think of when you were designing the product. In this case, the feature request needs to contain three essential pieces of information:

- What the feature should do

- Why this is important

- Who wants the feature

For anyone to implement the feature, you need to describe what it should do. This description should be as detailed as if you were writing a spec. For example, if your feature requires a new message box to pop up, you need to supply the text that you want to see in the message box. Without this level of detail, the developer who ultimately gets assigned the feature request won't know what to build (and the testers won't know what to test, and so on).

■**Tip** If you're the manager for a product, you should keep your specs up to date by incorporating any feature requests that are entered directly into FogBugz.

Justifying new features is particularly important. For many organizations, software development is a zero-sum game: with an announced release date, adding a new feature means throwing some other feature out (or reducing the product quality, which is usually a bad idea). You should be prepared to argue why your particular feature is essential. Does it take care of some unforeseen scenario where the application crashes or destroys data? Does it bring the product to feature parity with an important competitor? Is it something that will leapfrog all the competition and make the program sell like hotcakes?

Finally, make it clear who wants this feature. All other things being equal, a feature request from Joe Tester is less likely to meet the approval of management for this version than a feature request relayed from Mr. Megabux, your largest customer.

Keeping It Simple

Remember that I said that one of the underpinnings of FogBugz is to keep everything as simple as possible? To use the product successfully, you need to keep that rule in mind. FogBugz itself is customizable (after all, it's a set of ASP or PHP pages; there's nothing to prevent you from mucking about in the source code), but you shouldn't waste time fixing things that aren't broken. In addition to keeping the program itself simple, you also need to think about keeping your bug-tracking process simple. I'll close this chapter with a few concrete suggestions on how to do that.

On the application side, avoid the temptation to add new fields to FogBugz. Every month or so, somebody will come up with a great idea for a new field to put in the database. You get all kinds of clever ideas, for example, keeping track of the file where the bug was found; keeping track of how often the bug is reproducible; keeping track of how many times the bug occurred; keeping track of which exact versions of which DLLs were installed on the machine where the bug happened. It's very important not to give in to these ideas. If you do, your new bug entry screen will end up with a thousand fields that you need to supply, and nobody will want to input bug reports any more. For the bug database to work, everybody needs to use it, and if entering bugs "formally" is too much work, people will go around the bug database. At that point, your ability to track what's going on goes out the window. When bugs are swapped by e-mail, hallway conversation, and cocktail napkin, you can't trust the estimates coming out of FogBugz, you can't search effectively for duplicate bugs, and you're generally in trouble.

On the process side, you should consider training testers to write good bug reports. Meetings between the test team and the development team can also be helpful (that is, if your organization somehow enforces distance between these two teams, which I think is a bad idea anyhow).

A good tester will always try to reduce the repro steps to the minimal steps to reproduce; this is extremely helpful for the programmer who has to find the bug. Developers can also give the testers an idea of the sort of information that they find extraneous, and the sort that they find necessary, in bugs that have already been entered.

Keep track of versions on a fine-grained basis. Every build that goes off the build machine should have a unique version number. Testers need to report the version where they found a bug, and developers need to report the version where they fixed the bug. This avoids pain all around.

Everyone should be responsible for keeping the customers happy. Everyone on the team needs to at least dip into the discussion groups to see what customers are talking about, and should feel free to open cases based on discussion group comments. You may also want to have everyone review the e-mail inquiries that have ended up in the inbox project, and sort them to the correct project. This helps ensure a timely response to customers. For larger projects and teams, though, it's a better idea to have one person (or a small team of people) whose job it is to explicitly sort the incoming inquiries.

Summary

The story of every bug is a variation on this theme:

- Someone finds it and reports it.

- The bug gets bounced around from person to person until it finds the person who is really going to resolve it.

- When the bug is resolved, it goes back to the person who originally reported it for confirmation.

- If, and only if, they are satisfied with the resolution, they close the bug, and you never see it again.

In this chapter, you've seen how FogBugz enables you to work through this process with a minimum of overhead. You've also learned a little about how to use the system most effectively by writing good bug reports and feature requests, and by not cluttering the process up with unnecessary overhead.

If you've installed FogBugz, you're probably ready to dive in and start entering cases now. Great! But there's still plenty more to learn about FogBugz that might not be apparent at first. So after you get those first few cases cooking, read on. In the next chapter, I'll dig into case management in more detail, and show you some of the other tools that FogBugz has to offer.

■ ■ ■

CHAPTER 2

Managing Cases

Now that you've seen the high-level overview of FogBugz, you're ready to start working with cases related to your own products. But there's an art to working with cases effectively. You need to understand the categories of cases, where they come from, and their composition. FogBugz also offers more advanced facilities such as adding screenshots to cases and filtering cases to get just the ones that you need to work with at the moment. In this chapter, I'll show you how to manage cases easily and effectively.

The Three Categories of Cases

FogBugz supports three (and only three) categories of cases:

- Bugs

- Features

- Inquiries

Working with each of these is broadly similar, but there are differences. If you understand the purpose of each of these categories, you can do a better job of making cases useful to your whole team.

Bugs

Bugs are things that are wrong with the application. More precisely, a bug is something that the submitter *thinks is wrong* with the product. When you're training people to use FogBugz, it's important that you not scare them away from entering bugs. If you emphasize that bugs are for things that are actually wrong, you can set up a thought process among casual testers that goes like this: "Gosh, that looks like a bug to me. Maybe I should report it. But I haven't read the product spec. This is my first day working with the program. Maybe it's supposed to work that way. I'll wait. I can always report it later if I find out for sure it's a bug."

The end result of this sort of thinking is that the bug never gets entered—and therefore never gets resolved. Remember, developers can only resolve bugs that they know about. You should let your testers know that when in doubt, they should open a bug. It's a lot easier for the program manager to close off a bug as By Design than it is for them to deduce the existence of a rare bug that they were never told about.

Features

Features are things that should be (in the opinion of the submitter) added to the product. You can break down features further into two types. First, there are the features added by the product manager as a way to assign tasks to developers. These features will normally be developed from the product's spec, as you learned in Chapter 1. Developers don't usually have a choice about these features; they must be implemented.

The second type of feature comes from testers, users, managers, and other stakeholders who think they know what the product needs to make it more useful. These features have not been through the winnowing process of spec writing, and may or may not be realistic. New features from outside of the spec should first be assigned to the product manager, who can make the call as to whether they fit in this release, need to be postponed, or should never be implemented.

■**Caution** Sometimes you'll find developers who enter features and then assign those features to themselves as a way to remember things that they intend to work on. You should discourage this practice if you see it happening. The problem with this scenario is that one person is responsible for entering, resolving, and closing the entire feature, so the rest of the team has no visibility. Encourage developers to submit their features through program management like everyone else. The exception to this rule is in tracking tasks that don't need to be visible to anyone else; for example, developers might choose to maintain their own to-do lists in FogBugz rather than by putting TODO comments in code. When in doubt, err on the side of making bugs visible to more than one person.

Inquiries

Finally, inquiries represent questions from customers or other stakeholders. If you've set up an e-mail mailbox for your project, anyone who knows the address of that mailbox can enter an inquiry. Some inquiries may be answered by customer service people (for example, with the URL of a knowledge base article that explains how to perform the task that the customer asked about). Others will be reclassified as bugs or features.

■**Tip** Reserving inquiries for cases that come from completely outside of the project team gives you an easy way to track the volume of feedback that you're receiving.

■**Note** No one will enforce this division of features, bugs, and inquiries on you. If you decide that it makes more sense for your team to use inquiries to represent less severe bugs and general internal questions, that's fine. Just make sure that the whole team knows how things should be split up.

Where Do Cases Come From?

As you know, FogBugz stores all of its cases in a database. But where do those cases come from? You may think of FogBugz as a strictly Web-driven application, but in fact there are five distinct avenues that cases can take to get into the system:

- Web interface

- E-mail

- Discussion group

- ScoutSubmit

- Import

Let's look at each of these in turn.

Entering Cases via the Web

In the typical FogBugz installation, most cases come in via the Web interface, which is shown in Figure 2-1. Depending on how your server is set up, this interface may or may not be available to customers. Most organizations will choose to host their FogBugz server in such a way that you need to log on to enter cases, so that customers without an account will not have access to this screen.

You can normally create a new case this way by filling out less than a dozen fields (there are more than a dozen fields on the page, but some, such as Estimate, aren't likely to be filled in by the person submitting the case). I'll discuss some of these fields in more detail later in the chapter in the section "The Parts of a Case."

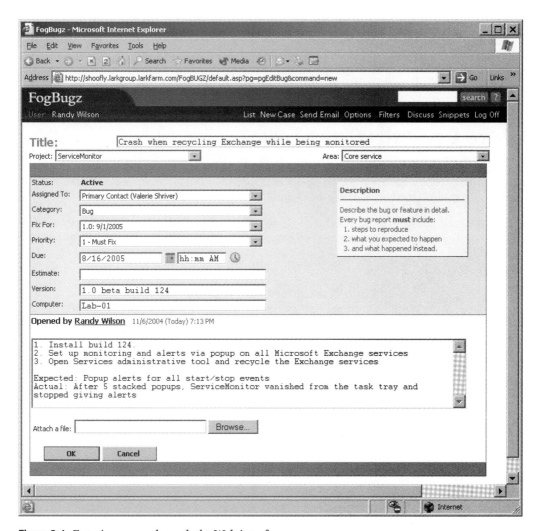

Figure 2-1. *Entering a case through the Web interface*

Entering Cases via E-Mail

Cases from customers and others outside of your development group are likely to get into the system via e-mail. Most FogBugz administrators will want to set up one or more mailboxes to receive incoming cases. Figure 2-2 shows a typical case that arrived via e-mail, before anyone from the project team worked on it.

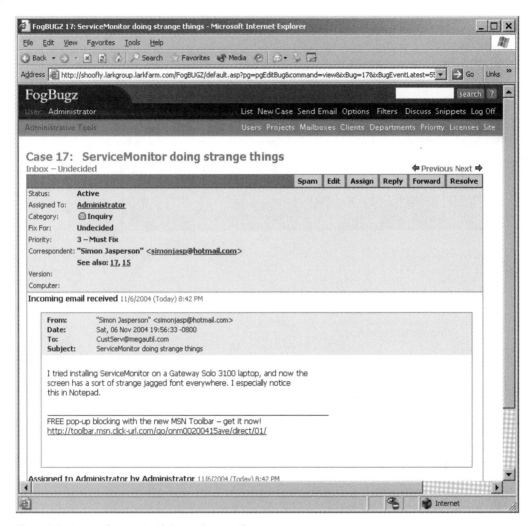

Figure 2-2. *A case that arrived through e-mail*

Note that the category for this case is automatically set to Inquiry. The FogBugz administrator can also define defaults for the other fields in the case. There are also a couple of extra buttons for the case; with one click, you can dismiss an e-mailed case as spam, or send a reply to the sender.

Note I'll discuss using FogBugz with e-mail extensively in Chapter 5.

Tip Cases entered from e-mail will have a Reply button that sends mail to the original sender.

Entering Cases via Discussion Group

FogBugz can also leverage discussion groups to create new cases in the system. This feature lets you tap the collective knowledge and ideas of all your users. When a registered user of FogBugz logs on and goes to a discussion group topic, they'll see New Case links for each message, as shown in Figure 2-3.

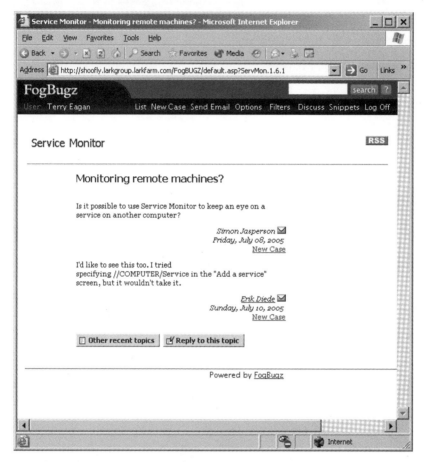

Figure 2-3. *Reading a discussion group while logged on*

Clicking the New Case link automatically creates a bug from the selected discussion group message. The title of the bug will be set to the title of the discussion group thread, and the contents of the message will be pasted into the bug description. The person porting the message to a case can make any other necessary changes (such as setting the project and area) and then click OK to create the case. Figure 2-4 shows a case created from one of the messages shown in Figure 2-3.

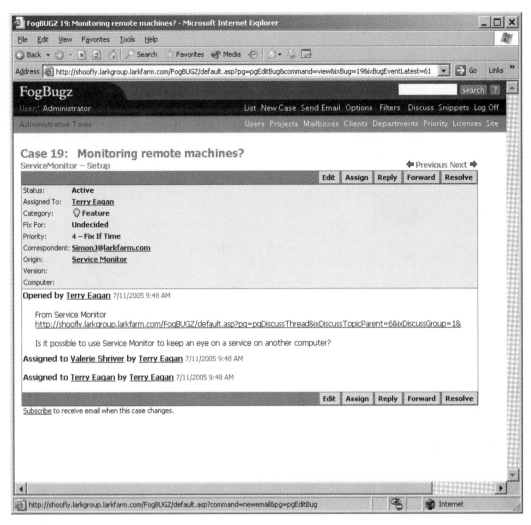

Figure 2-4. *Case that started as a discussion group message*

Tip Cases entered from discussion groups will have a Reply button that sends mail to the original discussion group poster, as well as a hyperlink to the discussion group posting.

Entering Cases via ScoutSubmit

Your FogBugz installation contains a file named ScoutSubmit.asp (or ScoutSubmit.php if you're using the Mac or Unix version). This file exists to take cases via a standard HTTP POST mechanism. If you make ScoutSubmit.asp visible to the public, then anyone who can create a properly formatted request can enter a bug. The ScoutSample.zip folder in your FogBugz installation demonstrates two possible approaches to allowing case entry via ScoutSubmit.

Figure 2-5 shows ScoutSample.html, which accepts results in an HTML form and packages them up for sending to ScoutSubmit.

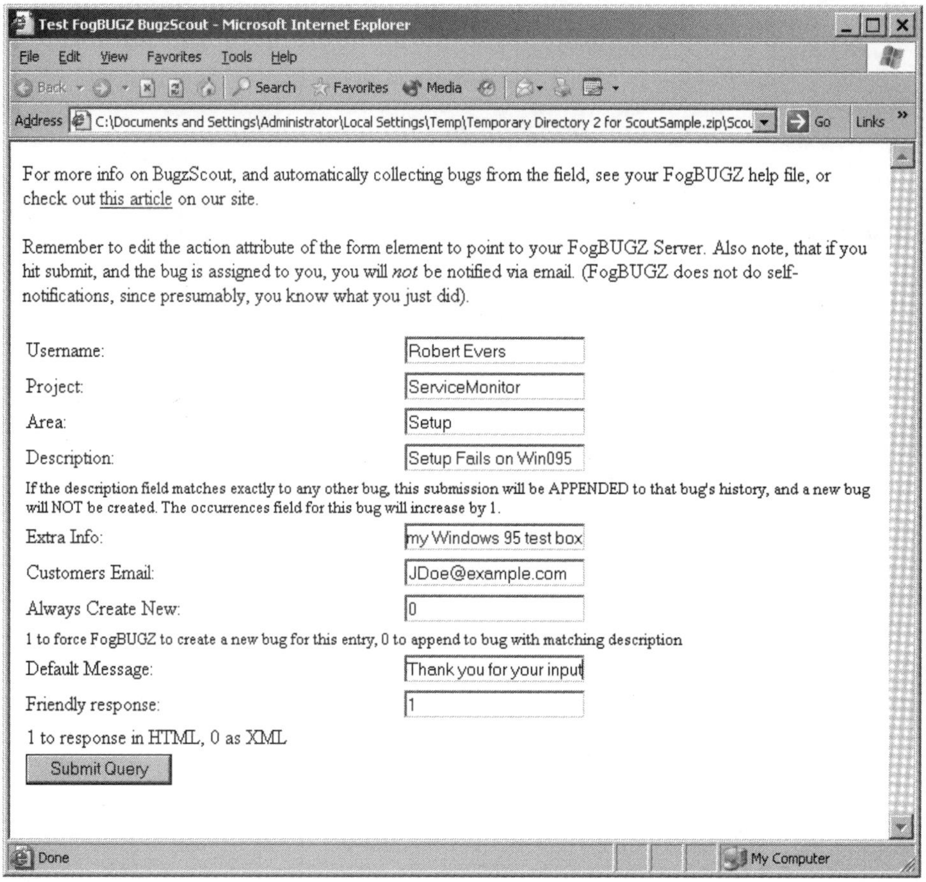

Figure 2-5. *Entering a case via ScoutSample.html*

Of course, ScoutSample.html exists only to show you the parameters that you can submit in the HTTP POST. You ought to customize this page for your own uses. When you do so, you'll probably want to use hidden fields for some of the data, such as the default message to return to the submitter and the FogBugz username.

The corresponding case for Figure 2-5 is shown in Figure 2-6. Note that there are several special features to a case submitted this way:

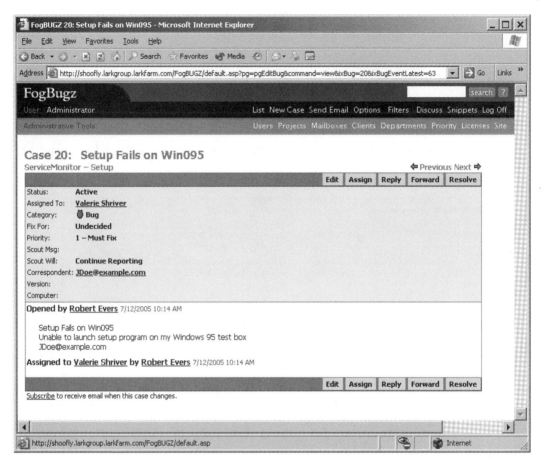

Figure 2-6. *A case entered via ScoutSubmit*

The Reply button sends a message to the e-mail address that was supplied via ScoutSubmit.

The Scout Msg field lets you enter a message to be sent back to anyone else who reports the same bug. You could use this to send workaround instructions or a suggestion to upgrade to a later build.

The Scout Will field lets you choose whether to accept future duplicates of the same bug. If you leave this set to Continue Reporting, new reports with the same title will be appended to the original case. If you change it to Stop Reports, additional reports will be discarded.

The other tool FogBugz includes to work with ScoutSubmit is BugzScout, an ActiveX control designed to construct the proper HTTP request. You can use this control in any application that can host ActiveX, which is a pretty broad range. This lets you add automated or manual case entry directly to your applications. For instance, you could implement Add a Bug as a menu item in your next beta build. The FogBugz installation includes C++ and C# examples of using BugzScout.

Note For more details on BugzScout coding, see Appendix B.

Importing Cases

Finally, you may need to import cases from another bug-tracking system. If you're using the open-source Bugzilla system (http://www.bugzilla.org/), then there's a solution built into FogBugz. Locate the importBugzilla.asp file in your FogBugz folder, and open it in your browser, as shown in Figure 2-7.

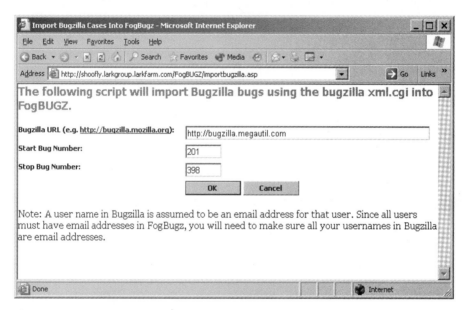

Figure 2-7. *Preparing to import bugs from Bugzilla*

If you're using something other than Bugzilla, things can be trickier, because you're basically on your own. However, you do have one advantage: everything is stored in a single SQL Server, Access, or MySQL database, and the field names are sensible. So if your existing bug-tracking tool is backed by a database, you can use the tool of your choice (such as SQL Server Data Transformation Services) to move the data from the old database to the new database.

The Parts of a Case

Now that you know all the different ways to open a case, it's time to look at the fields that define a case in more detail. Figure 2-8 shows a typical just-opened case. The developer got e-mail telling her that she'd just been assigned a new case, and she's opened it and clicked the Edit button.

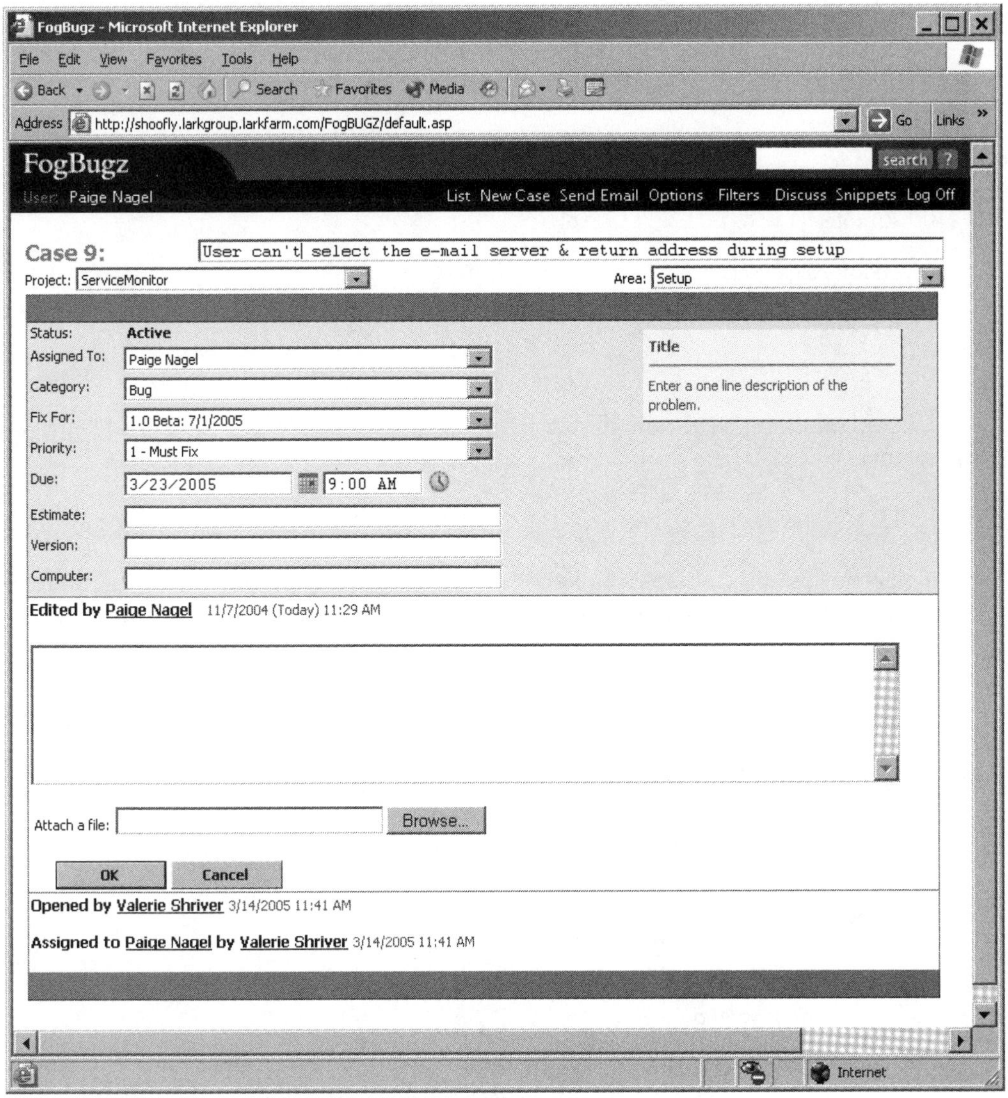

Figure 2-8. *Editing a case*

As you can see, there are quite a number of fields that can be edited for a case:

- Title
- Project
- Area
- Assigned To

- Category

- Fix For

- Priority

- Due date and time

- Estimate

- Version

- Computer

- Notes

Some of these may be obvious to you; others are likely to be a little bit obscure. I'll review each of them in turn.

Title

Getting a good title for a case is absolutely critical. When you're looking at a list of bugs, the title is the best information that you have about the case's contents. Although it's possible to edit the title, you should do so with care; other people on your team may be keeping an eye on the bug and remembering it by title.

Tip If you want to track a particular bug, you should use FogBugz's e-mail subscription feature, discussed in Chapter 5.

Some guidelines for writing good case titles:

- Keep them short. About 80 characters is all that you can depend on people seeing on low-resolution screens.

- Make the title descriptive of the case. In some cases (such as the one shown in Figure 2-8) the title can be so clear that the case doesn't need any further description.

- Titles for bugs should state a problem: "CD-ROM fails to function after installing software."

- Titles for features should specify what to implement: "Add popup Unicode conversion table."

- Avoid any language that you wouldn't use in face-to-face conversation with stake-holders in the project. "This software is lousy junk" may reflect your feelings when you hit a bug that causes loss of data, but it's not a good bug title.

Project and Area

The choices in the Project and Area drop-down lists are set up by the FogBugz administrators, and the lists of choices can't be changed while you're editing a case. This is a good thing, because it keeps these lists from growing as everyone puts in their own idea of what the choices should be. When you're entering and editing cases, it should be fairly obvious which choices to make in these lists (assuming your administrators did a good job of setting things up).

■**Note** I'll discuss setting up projects and areas in detail in Chapter 3.

Assigned To

The Assigned To drop-down list includes everyone who's a user of your FogBugz installation. You can assign a case to another user in three ways:

- When you're editing the case, you can choose a user in the drop-down list.

- Instead of editing a case, you can click the Assign To button, which lets you select a new user and add notes without making any other changes.

- When you resolve a case, it's automatically assigned to the user who entered the case in the first place.

The first entry in the drop-down list will always be the primary contact for the project to which the case is assigned. If you're entering a new case, this is the person to whom FogBugz will automatically assign the case.

Sometimes, people will want to share the ownership of a case among multiple people. In principle this sounds good, but in real life, if a task or bug is owned by more than one person, it is owned by nobody and gets neglected. That is why FogBugz is written to assume one person per bug.

On the other hand, sometimes you have a team of people who are equally capable of working on a set of tasks or bugs, and you want to be able to assign the bug to that team for a while before you decide who is going to work on it. There are two ways to do this.

The traditional way is simply to assign it to the team lead. The team lead winds up with a bunch of bugs that they are not going to work on personally, but which they haven't yet passed out to the team members.

Another good way is to create an account in FogBugz for the whole team in addition to personal accounts. You can assign bugs to this virtual account, and tell the team members that when they have a chance they should go through the bugs assigned to their team and then personally assign to themselves any bugs which they are ready to work on. For example, you might create a virtual account called "New Bugs," with e-mail notification turned off on that account, and set that as the project owner. The team members responsible for assigning bugs could each check the bugs assigned to "New Bugs" regularly, using a saved filter, and assign the bugs to individuals.

If there are several people who need to be notified whenever something changes about a bug, they can all subscribe to the bug by clicking the small link at the bottom of the bug report.

Category

The Category drop-down list is where you identify the case as a bug, feature, or inquiry. It makes sense to edit this in some scenarios:

- If the product manager or developer determines that a bug isn't in the scope of the original spec, it can be reclassified as a feature.

- Inquiries from customers will often be sorted into bugs and features as the development team works with them.

Fix For

The Fix For drop-down list lets you choose a release for which this bug needs to be fixed (or this feature needs to be implemented). Like projects and areas, releases are set up by your FogBugz administrators. Usually the value in this field will be assigned by the project manager, or possibly by some triage committee. There's nothing built into the software to prevent developers from pushing back their own Fix For values to gain time to fix bugs, but managers are likely to notice when bugs start piling up.

Priority

FogBugz allows you to assign each case a priority from 1 (the most important cases to resolve) to 7 (cases that don't need to be resolved). The FogBugz administrator can change the wording of the priorities, but the scale will always run from 1 to 7. Experience has shown that most people can't distinguish between more gradations than that. If you're entering a bug and unsure which priority to assign it, choose a higher priority. That will get the attention of managers and developers, who can always downgrade the case if they disagree with you.

Due Date and Time

Although each case should have a Fix For value, you probably don't want a sudden avalanche of fixes descending on your application's source code the night before a release. That's why you can assign finer-grained due dates using these two controls. Typically, the project manager will use these controls to even out workflow, dictate when features should be implemented, and prioritize work.

You can click the calendar icon to select a date from a calendar or the clock icon to select a time from a drop-down list. FogBugz also understands a variety of informal ways of specifying a date or time. You can type phrases like these in the Due Date textbox, and FogBugz will replace them with the correct date and time when you tab to another control:

- today

- tomorrow

- the day after tomorrow

- in 3 days

- in 1 week

- Tuesday

- next Friday

- march 1

- 12/30 (or 30.12 outside the USA)

- 12/30/2006 (or 30.12.2006 outside the USA)

- June

You can also type some things in the Time textbox:

- noon

- midnight

- now

- in 1 hour

- in 3 hours

Estimate

The Estimate field is an essential part of using FogBugz as a project-tracking tool. Normally, the person who creates the case will leave this field blank, to be filled in by the developer. The developer should estimate the time that it will take to close the case and fill this in as soon as they look at the case. Estimates are in days and hours, and you can use the format 6h or 3d8h to enter them.

After you've entered an estimate, FogBugz presents some additional controls in this area, as shown in Figure 2-9. You can't change the original estimate, but you can reestimate the total work by entering a value in the Current textbox, and show how much effort has been expended in the Elapsed textbox.

Figure 2-9. *Editing an estimate*

■Note For more information on using estimates, see Chapter 4.

Version and Computer

The version and computer fields accept free-form text. Typically, the person who originally enters a bug will put the software version where the bug appeared in the Version field, and the name of their computer in the Computer field. Knowing the name of the computer can help track what's going on when you're running automated tests in a lab, for example.

■**Tip** You should assign a version number to every build of your software and make sure it's easy for testers to find (perhaps by putting it on the help menu or in the title bar). This will help ensure accurate use of the Version field.

If you decide that you don't require these two pieces of information, your FogBugz administrator can rename Version and Computer to capture any two other pieces of information. For example, you might decide that you don't care about computers, but you do care about the operating system of the computer where the case was reported. That's fine; just have the administrator rename the Computer field to Operating System and you're ready to go.

■**Note** For more details on customizing these fields, see Chapter 3.

■**Tip** New installations of FogBugz 4.0 will have these fields turned off by default. If you don't see them, your administrator can turn them on in site settings.

Notes

Finally, the free-form notes field serves as a scratchpad and history area for the case. As different people work with the case, FogBugz makes notes of actions such as resolving the case, reactivating it, or closing it. Figure 2-10 shows what the notes might look like in a case that's bounced around a bit.

When you're deciding how much detail to add in notes for a case, remember that these notes are part of your institutional memory. If the question "Why did we do it that way?" comes up, it's nice to be able to look back and see the debate as it happened. It's especially important to record the details if you're responsible for a decision that might be controversial in the future. For example, if you resolve a bug report as "Won't Fix," be sure to explain your reasoning in the notes. This will help keep the original reporter from just reopening the bug on the theory that you didn't understand it.

■**Note** Because FogBugz cases can be linked directly to source code, there's no need to copy code or comments from the actual source code into the notes. See Chapter 6 for more information on how to tie FogBugz together with your source code control system.

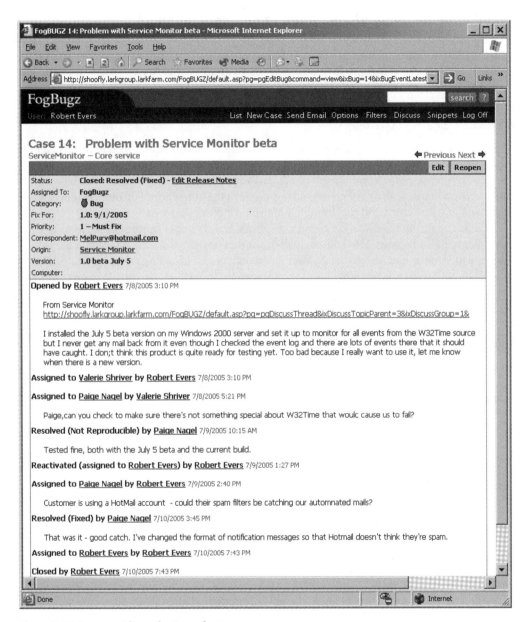

Figure 2-10. *A case with a selection of notes*

Using Screenshots and Attached Files

Cases in FogBugz aren't limited to the words that you type in. You can also add files to cases to make it easier for the developer to understand what's going on. FogBugz includes its own dedicated screenshot tool. For other files, there's a general-purpose way to attach files to any case.

Taking Screenshots

Sometimes, describing a bug in words is tedious. Other times it's simply impossible. If there's a subtle problem with control rendering on one version of Windows, for example, you don't want to have to specify the number of pixels that you think are wrong on the vertical lines. A much better choice is to take a picture and attach it to the bug report. Fortunately, FogBugz supports its own Screenshot tool for either Mac or Windows desktops.

To set up the Screenshot tool, log on to FogBugz and click the Capture Screenshots link on your FogBugz home page. This will take you to another page from which you can do the actual download for your operating system. After downloading and installing the program, you'll have a bug icon on your Windows taskbar, as shown in Figure 2-11, or a bug icon on your Mac menu bar, as shown in Figure 2-12.

Figure 2-11. *FogBugz Screenshot program on Windows*

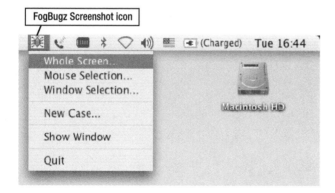

Figure 2-12. *FogBugz Screenshot program on Mac OS X*

The Mac and the Windows version of the Screenshot tool are almost identical but differ in small ways.

After you've installed the Screenshot tool, click the bug icon to perform a capture. A single click is all it takes. On Windows, the Screenshot tool captures the active window by default, as shown in Figure 2-13.

On Mac OS X, select the bug icon in the menu bar at the top of the screen, and then choose Whole Screen, Mouse Selection (for just part of the screen), or Window Selection (to grab a specific window). If you choose Window Selection, the cursor will change to a camera, and then you can highlight and select the window you want, as shown in Figure 2-14.

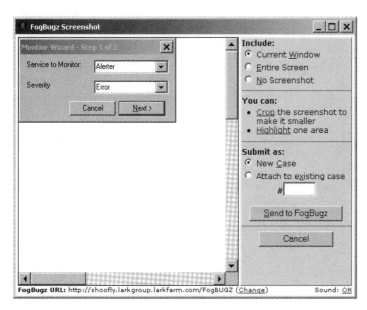

Figure 2-13. *Taking a screenshot on Windows*

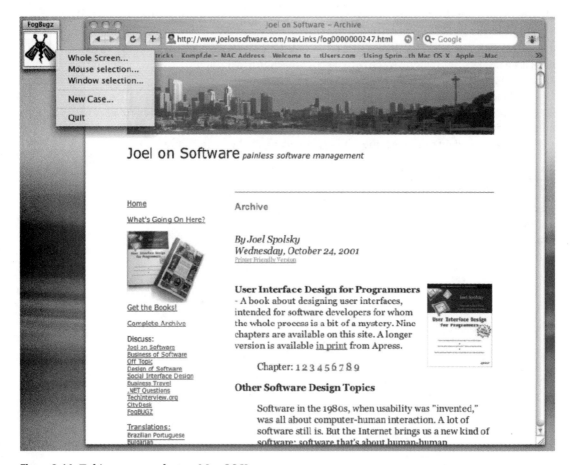

Figure 2-14. *Taking a screenshot on Mac OS X*

After you take a screenshot, you can use the hyperlinks to the right of the work area to modify the screenshot. On Windows, you can crop the screenshot (making it smaller) or highlight an area to illustrate where the bug appears (which surrounds it with a bold red rectangle). On Mac OS X, you have to crop before you take the screenshot by choosing Mouse Selection, but you can still highlight the screenshot after you take it. Then you can decide whether to submit the screenshot as a new case or to attach it to an existing case. To attach the screenshot to an existing case, you must know the case number. Figure 2-15 shows a case with a screenshot; the screenshot shows up directly in the browser when you view the case.

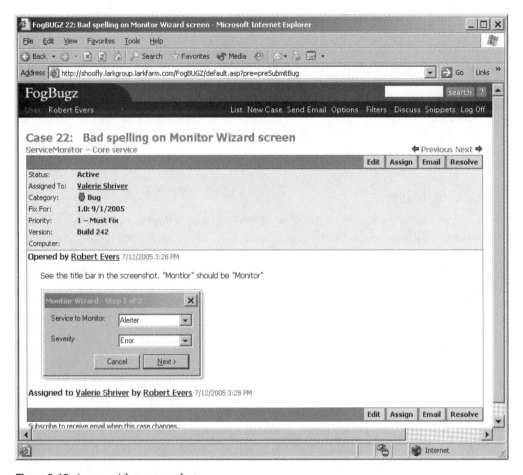

Figure 2-15. *A case with a screenshot*

Right-clicking the Windows Screenshot tool brings up a menu with the following options:

- *Capture Screenshot Now*: This is equivalent to just clicking the tool.

- *About FogBugz Screenshot*: Shows information about the program.

- *New Case*: Opens a browser window ready to enter a new case. This is the fastest way to start a new case if you have the Screenshot tool running.

- *Exit*: Removes the Screenshot tool from the taskbar and closes the application.

Right-clicking the Macintosh Screenshot tool brings up a slightly different set of menu options:

- *Whole Screen*: Captures the entire desktop window.

- *Mouse Selection*: Captures a specific piece of the desktop.

- *Window Selection*: Captures a specific window.

- *New Case*: Opens a browser window ready to enter a new case. This is the fastest way to start a new case if you have the Screenshot tool running.

- *Quit*: Removes the Screenshot tool from the menu bar and closes the application.

Attaching Files

When you're editing any case in FogBugz, you'll find an Attach a File control directly under the active Notes area. You can type in the name of a file here, or use the Browse button next to it to locate a file on your hard drive. When you click OK to save your edits, FogBugz will also upload the file and store it with the case. If you browse to a case that includes an attached file, you'll see a paper clip icon and the file name. If the file is recognized as an image type, such as .jpg or .gif, it will be shown as part of the case. Click either the icon or the file name to open the file.

Attachments are useful for a number of purposes:

- To collect configuration files specific to a particular test machine

- To store log files of the actions leading up to a case

- To hold output files that show a problem

Caution If you allow public access to your FogBugz site, you need to exercise caution in clicking links to attached files. FogBugz will do its best to protect you from dangerous file extensions (such as .exe, .scr, and .pif) by adding .safe to the end of the file name. If you click one of these files, your browser will prompt you to save the file instead of immediately executing it.

Linking Cases

Sometimes you want to indicate that two cases are related. For example:

- You might determine that a case is a duplicate of an existing case.

- A bug might be a regression of a feature that was previously implemented.

- A case might incorporate incidental suggestions from another case.

FogBugz offers two ways to link cases. First, you can create a link between cases just by typing the word "case" or the word "bug" followed by a case number. For example, Figure 2-16 shows a bug entered as a follow-up to another bug. Note that the words "Case 19" have been automatically hyperlinked by FogBugz.

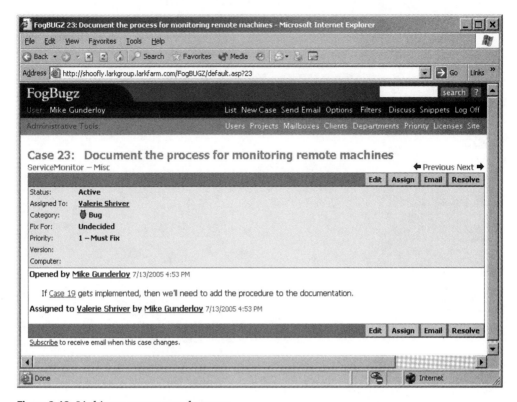

Figure 2-16. *Linking a case to another case*

Any time FogBugz creates a link, it makes the link bidirectional. When you open the linked case, you'll see that it lists a related case in its fields, as shown in Figure 2-17.

Note Linking is not transitive. That is, if you link case 23 to case 19, and case 42 to case 19, then case 19 will show both case 23 and case 42 as related cases, but case 23 and case 42 will not be related to each other.

The other way to create a link between two cases is to resolve a case as a duplicate. When you resolve a case as a duplicate, FogBugz will prompt you for the number of the duplicate case. Both cases will then show up as duplicates of each other when you browse to them in the future. This is especially useful when the cases seem to be different at first glance but have the same underlying cause.

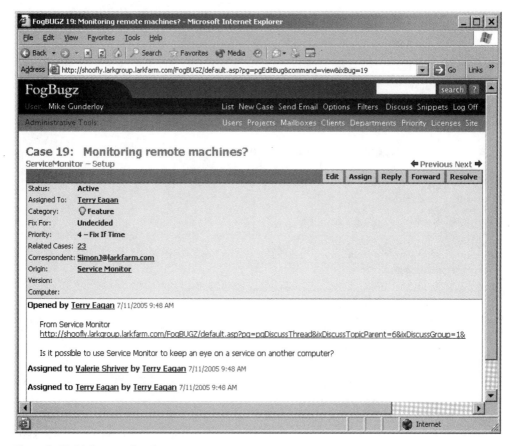

Figure 2-17. *Link to a related case*

Filtering Cases

If your team is diligent about using FogBugz, you'll quickly go from having dozens of cases in the system to hundreds to thousands. Trying to find one case in that huge pile would be difficult. Fortunately, there's an easy way to focus on just the cases you need. FogBugz supports the notion of a filter; at any given time, FogBugz only shows you a list of the cases that match your current filter.

Selecting a Filter

When you log on to FogBugz, the right side of your home page shows a list of saved filters under the "Show Me" title, as shown in Figure 2-18. By default, this list will only include Inbox (a filter that shows inquiries in the Inbox that are waiting to be processed) and My Cases (a filter that shows all open cases assigned to the current user). The user in Figure 2-18 also has several custom filters on her list.

Figure 2-18. *A list of filters*

Clicking a filter opens a list of cases that match that filter. For example, Figure 2-19 shows the cases that match the All open SM cases filter from Figure 2-18.

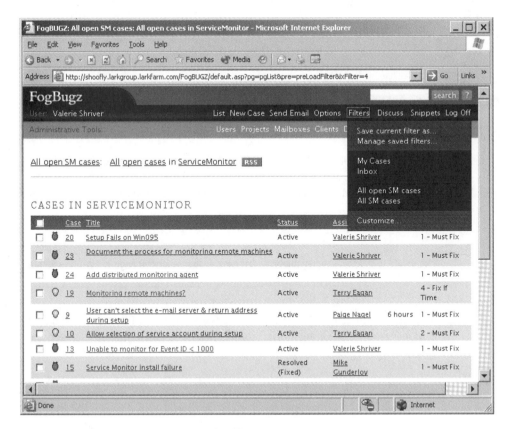

Figure 2-19. *Cases that match a particular filter*

You can also select a saved filter from the Filters menu at the top of the screen at any time to see the cases that match that filter. You don't need to return to the home page to select a new filter.

■Tip Clicking the List shortcut in the menu always returns you to your most recent filter.

Modifying Filters

Filters are made to be easy to change. Suppose you're looking at the open cases for a particular project, and you can't find the case that you're looking for. Perhaps someone has closed it. At the top of the list of cases, you'll see information about the current filter. First comes the name of the filter ("All open SM cases" in Figure 2-19). Next comes a series of conditions showing the parts that make up this filter. Click any of the underlined words to pop up a menu that lets you modify the current filter, as shown in Figure 2-20.

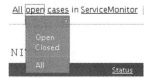

Figure 2-20. *Modifying a filter*

For example, clicking Open gives you a menu that lets you choose open cases, closed cases, or all cases. To switch from looking at open cases to looking at closed cases, just click Closed in the menu. FogBugz will change the filter and refresh the screen to show you the cases that meet the new filter.

■Tip If you click one of the filtering links by mistake, just click anywhere on the page to close the menu.

You can also add additional conditions by clicking the name of the filter. This will display a menu that includes all of the possible filtering conditions. Click one of the plus signs to see the choices in that condition, and then click a choice to add it to the filter. Figure 2-21 shows this menu.

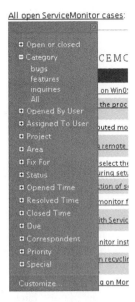

Figure 2-21. *Adding a condition to a filter*

You can set up filter conditions for just about anything about a case. The available filtering choices include the following:

- Open or closed cases

- Cases without estimates

- Cases to which you are subscribed

- Cases in a specific category

- Cases from a specific project

- Cases from a specific area

- Cases opened by a specific person

- Cases assigned to a specific person

- Cases with a particular status ("Active," "Resolved (Duplicate)," and so on)

- Cases with a specific Fix For value

- Cases with a specific priority, with a priority at least equal to a specific priority, or with a priority at most equal to a specific priority

- Cases opened in a particular time period

- Cases resolved in a particular time period

- Cases closed in a particular time period

- Cases due in a particular time period

- Cases e-mailed from or to a particular correspondent (or, since you can use partial matching here, from a specific domain)

- Cases with a specific version

- Cases with a specific computer

You can also choose to sort the filter on up to three fields and set a limit on the number of cases that the filter can return.

Clicking Customize at the bottom of the conditions list or selecting Customize from the Filters menu at the top of the screen will take you to the filter customization screen. This screen, shown in Figure 2-22, lets you make changes to the current filter by selecting from drop-down lists.

To apply changes from the filter customization screen and return to the list of bugs, click OK at the bottom of the screen. You can also use this screen to save the changes under a new name by supplying a name in the Save As box before you click OK. The newly saved filter will now show up in your Filters menu list and on your home page.

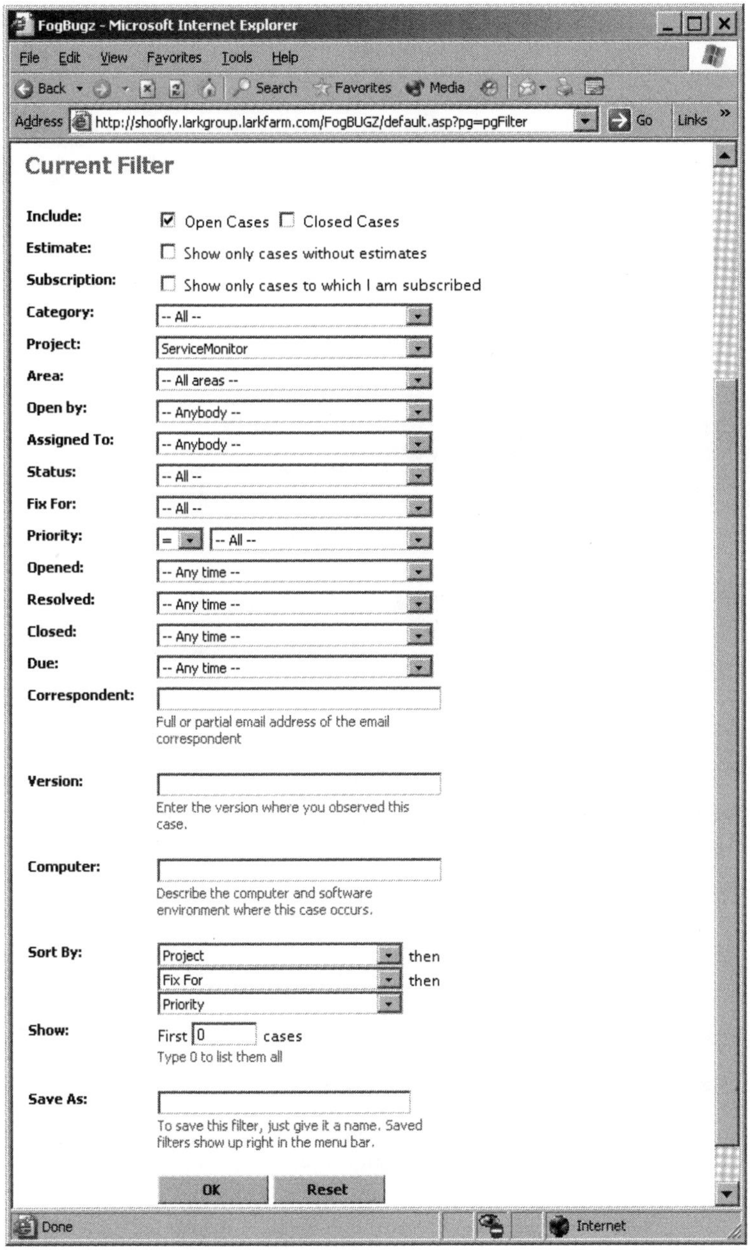

Figure 2-22. *Customizing a filter*

Saving, Managing, and Sharing Filters

In addition to saving filters from the filter customization screen, you can also save a filter directly from the list of cases. After you've tweaked a filter to get what you want, select Save Current Filter As from the Filters menu. You'll be prompted to fill in a filter name. Choose a name that describes the filter and click OK to add this filter to your list of saved filters.

Select Manage Saved Filters from the Filters menu to open the screen shown in Figure 2-23.

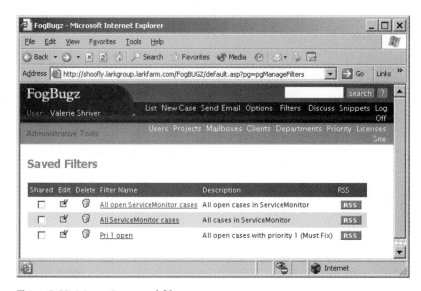

Figure 2-23. *Managing saved filters*

This screen shows you all of the custom filters that you've created. For each filter, you can perform these actions:

- Share the filter with the entire team by checking the Shared checkbox. The filter will now appear on everyone's list of filters. This checkbox is only available to FogBugz administrators.

- Edit the conditions for the filter by clicking the icon in the Edit column.

- Delete the filter by clicking the icon in the Delete column. There's no confirmation for this action, so be sure you really want to delete the filter before you click!

- View the cases that match the filter by clicking the filter name.

- View the RSS feed for the filter by clicking the RSS icon.

■**Note** You'll learn about RSS in Chapter 4.

Working with Filtered Cases

Often, you want to work through a list of cases—checking that they are assigned to the right person, reevaluating their priorities, and so on. FogBugz makes this easy by providing Next and Previous links in the top corner of each case, which show the next or previous case in your current filter. Thus, you don't have to keep going back to the full list to see each case.

Caution If you change the case's position in the filter while you work through the list, you may be confused by the behavior of the Next button. For example, if your filter lists cases in order of priority, and you change a case's priority to be higher, clicking Next will take you to a case you've already seen. The easiest way to prevent this is to use a stable sort order, for example, sort by Case ID number, which won't change as you work through the list.

Another thing that makes working with a long list of cases simpler is that FogBugz carefully coordinates with your Web browser to ensure that bugs you've already seen are shown in the "visited links" color (usually purple), while bugs you haven't seen are in the "unvisited links" color (usually blue). So if you're trying to look at just the new bugs that match a filter, click each blue link in turn until they're all purple.

FogBugz will even change the URL for any bug that changes after you last looked at the details. That way, if anything changes about a bug that you've already looked at, the link to that bug will appear blue again.

Searching for Cases

FogBugz also lets you find cases by searching for them—at least, if you can come up with a good search term. There's a search box at the upper left of every page in FogBugz. Type in a search term and click the Search button to search cases. By default, FogBugz searches the full text of every open case for the exact phrase that you typed. You can also open a separate search page by clicking the Search button without typing any text in the box. This page lets you limit your search to title text or include closed cases in the search.

Tip To quickly jump to a case, type the case number in the search box and hit Enter.

FogBugz uses a reasonably sophisticated full-text searching algorithm:

- To search for an exact phrase, enter the phrase ("rotary engine").

- To search for cases containing two words, but not necessarily an exact phrase, use AND ("screen AND repaint").

- To search for cases containing one or both of two words, use OR ("crash OR failure").

- To search for two words in close proximity, use NEAR ("string NEAR regedit").

- To search for words starting with a set of characters, use * as a wild card ("Subscri*").

Filtering done by the search process is temporary. If you click the List menu item, you'll go right back to looking at cases that match your current (pre-search) filter.

Using List and Grid Views

So far, I've shown you lists of cases in FogBugz's grid view. This is the default view for new users. Grid view shows you your cases in a grid that contains up to seven columns. Each column contains a particular piece of information on the case.

■**Note** In addition to the seven columns of information, there's a checkbox for selecting bugs. You'll learn about the use of this checkbox to modify cases in bulk in Chapter 3.

You can change the columns for grid view by clicking the Options menu item. Figure 2-24 shows the section of the Options page that lets you select the columns for your own personal grid.

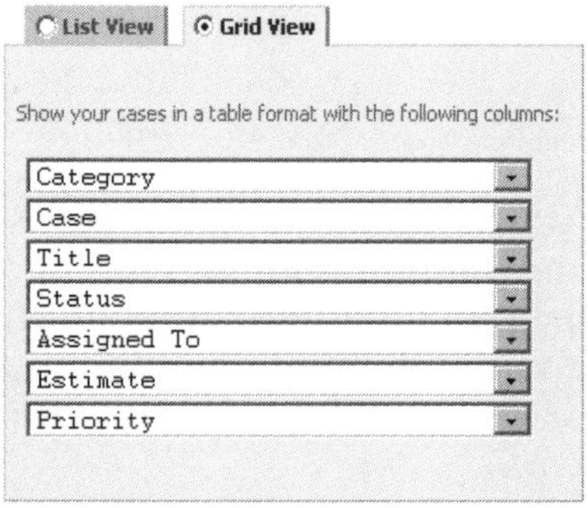

Figure 2-24. *Choosing columns for the grid view*

Alternatively, you may want to view cases in the newspaper-like list view. If you're viewing cases in grid view, click the Switch to List View link above the grid. This will change the list of bugs to list view, as shown in Figure 2-25, while preserving the current filter. Note that list view includes a Switch to Grid View link, so it's easy to get back.

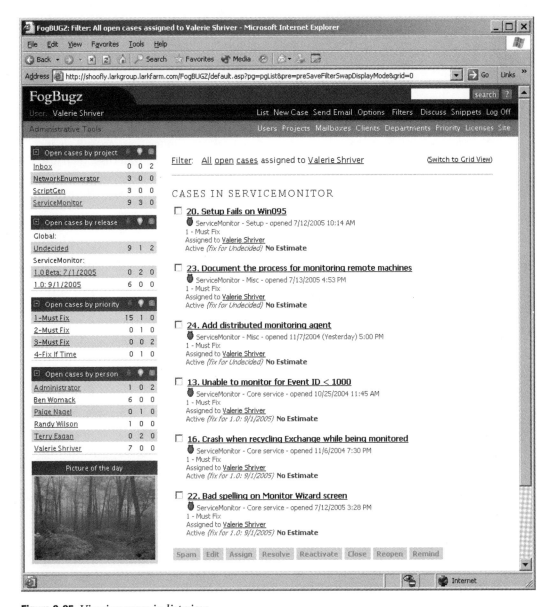

Figure 2-25. *Viewing cases in list view*

Each view has its own advantages. In grid view, it's easy to get an overall sense of the cases that match the current filter, and easy to scan down the list to find a case that you want. In list view, you have the benefit of seeing the summary boxes to the left of the list, which gives you a quick way to see how cases are distributed among projects, releases, priorities, and persons. Plus, in list view you also get to see the picture of the day.

Tip If you'd like list view to be your default, go to the Options page, click the List View tab next to the list of grid columns, and click OK.

Being a Good FogBugz Citizen

At this point you've seen many of the capabilities of FogBugz (though there are still plenty more things to learn in the rest of the book!). There's more to working with cases than just understanding the mechanics of FogBugz, though. To conclude this chapter, I'll offer some advice on how testers, developers, and managers should work with FogBugz to ensure a smooth-running operation.

Working with FogBugz As a Tester

As a tester working with FogBugz, you should

- Carefully choose descriptive titles for new cases.

- Prevent duplicate bugs by searching for existing cases before entering new ones.

- Include the three essential parts (reproduction steps, expected behavior, actual behavior) for every bug.

- Experiment to come up with the simplest possible set of reproduction steps.

- Confirm the resolution of bugs that are assigned back to you in a timely manner.

Working with FogBugz As a Developer

As a developer working with FogBugz, you should

- Review new cases assigned to you quickly so you can ask for more information if necessary.

- Not resolve bugs as "Not Reproducible" without checking with the tester first.

- Not resolve bugs as "Won't Fix" or "By Design" without the product manager's approval.

- Have a tester enter any bugs that you find, so that someone other than yourself will be in the loop as the bug is resolved.

- Use the source code control features of FogBugz to associate code fixes with bug fixes.

- Keep time estimates up to date.

- Keep case priorities in mind as you set your schedule.

Working with FogBugz As a Manager

As a manager working with FogBugz, you should

- Use FogBugz to assign features, so that they can be tracked like other cases.

- Quickly review new cases so you can assign them to the proper developer.

- Set up filters that allow you to track activity in the projects that you're responsible for.

- Set up filters for very old cases to warn you of potential trouble spots.

Summary

In this chapter, you learned how you can work with FogBugz on a day-to-day basis. You learned about the different categories of cases and the different ways in which a case can get to FogBugz. You also saw the parts of a case and learned which information should be entered where. I also demonstrated some of the useful tools that FogBugz provides for your daily work: screenshots, filters, and links.

You might be wondering at this point where some of the choices in FogBugz come from. For example, who chooses the projects and areas that are available to you when you enter a new case? For the answer, turn to the next chapter, where I'll cover some of the customization that your FogBugz administrator can do to the product.

■ ■ ■

CHAPTER 3

Making FogBugz Work for You

No software package is perfect for every user right out of the box—not even FogBugz! By now, you know how to work effectively with FogBugz once it's all set up, but I haven't yet discussed customization. The good news is that FogBugz allows you to customize a wide variety of things about your installation to make it work the way you need it to. In this chapter, I'll review the various administrative tasks involved in fine-tuning FogBugz to be right for your own project management.

Setting Up Users and Groups

When you first install FogBugz, a single user is already set up as the FogBugz administrator—conveniently named "Administrator." This initial user does not count against your FogBugz license count. No matter how many licenses you purchase, you always get an administrator account for free. So if you have 12 people using FogBugz, and one of them will primarily function as an administrator, you only need to purchase 11 licenses.

You'll certainly want to create other users, though. One of the strengths of FogBugz is its ability to track who has done what on any given case, and you can't do that if everyone is logging in as the same user.

Creating Users

Any FogBugz administrator can create a new user by selecting the Users item on the Administrative Tools bar. This opens the current user list, as shown in Figure 3-1.

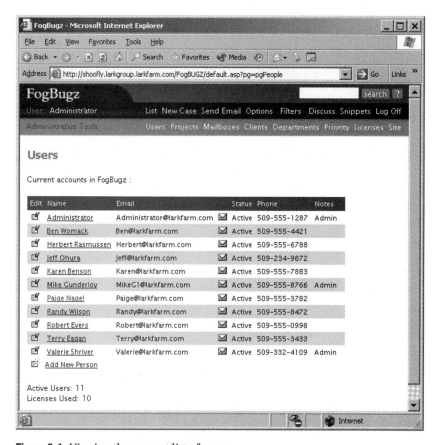

Figure 3-1. *Viewing the current list of users*

Click the Add New Person link at the bottom of this screen to add a new user. This opens up a blank form that you can fill in to create the new user account. You need to provide ten pieces of information to create a new user:

- The full name of the user. This is the name that FogBugz will display throughout the application.

- The e-mail address for the user. If the user has more than one e-mail address, and they want all FogBugz e-mail sent to all of their addresses, enter them separated by commas.

- The user's phone number. This is displayed on the user list in case someone needs to contact the user outside of the system for more information.

- Whether this user should receive e-mail notifications. You should almost always leave e-mail notifications turned on. If you turn them off, the user won't be notified when they're assigned a case in the system.

- Whether this user should receive escalation reports. Escalation reports, sent once a day by FogBugz, list all of the cases that are past due or due that day. You'll learn more about escalation reports in Chapter 4.

- Whether this user is an administrator. I'll discuss administrators further in the next section of this chapter.

- Whether this particular user is active. Your license count limits the number of active users you have, but you can also have any number of inactive users who can't log on. You'll almost always want new users to be active when you first create them, unless you're preparing for new licenses that you haven't purchased yet.

- The snippet activation key for the user. FogBugz supports inserting snippets of saved text by typing the name of the snippet and pressing this key. You'll learn more about snippets in Chapter 5.

- The columns to display on this user's list of cases. You learned about selecting columns in Chapter 2.

- The user's password.

When you've filled in all of the required information, click OK to create the new user. Assuming that you're not trying to exceed your license count, FogBugz will create the user immediately. If you do happen to exceed your license count, FogBugz will append a warning to the user list, as shown in Figure 3-2.

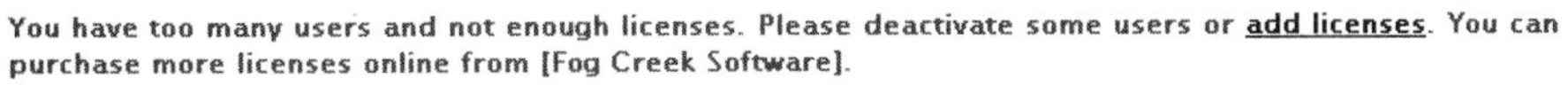

You have too many users and not enough licenses. Please deactivate some users or **add licenses**. You can purchase more licenses online from [Fog Creek Software].

Figure 3-2. *Warning from exceeding the license count*

If you don't have more licenses to install, you'll need to make some users inactive. To do so, click a user name in the user list or click the edit icon next to the user name. Either way, you'll end up at the options page for that user. Set the status for the user to inactive and click OK.

Note FogBugz doesn't let you delete users because that would potentially leave a hole in the history of existing cases.

The options page also lets administrators edit the information for any user. A user who is not an administrator can use the Options link in the FogBugz menu to edit some of their own information:

- E-mail address

- Phone number

- E-mail notifications

- Escalation reports

- Snippet activation key

- Display columns

- Password

Users who are not administrators can't edit the information for other users. In fact, if you're not an administrator, you can't even view the list of users. You can, however, get information on any particular user who has worked with a case that you're interested in. Just click the user's name anywhere in the case to get that user's information, as shown in Figure 3-3.

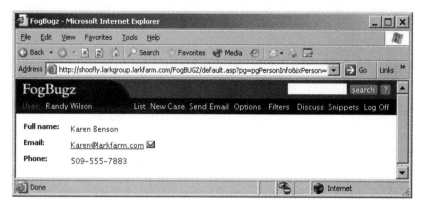

Figure 3-3. *Public information on a user*

The Power of FogBugz Administrators

Any FogBugz user can be made into an administrator. You can have as many administrators as you want (up to your total number of licensed users plus one). You've already seen some of the things that only administrators can do. Here are the abilities that are reserved for administrators:

- Configure and add users, and change their passwords (though users can also change their own passwords).

- Set up projects.

- Set up areas.

- Set up releases.

- Set up clients.

- Set up departments.

- Customize the working schedule.

- Configure all aspects of the FogBugz installation.

- Install new licenses purchased from Fog Creek.

Also, all administrators receive a copy of the e-mail that is sent when users choose the Email your FogBugz Administrators option on the Help menu. It's easy to tell when you're logged on as an administrator: you'll see the Administrative Tools bar at the top of the screen along with the regular set of tools for all users.

■**Note** FogBugz doesn't support creating groups of users, but you can get some of the benefits of groups by working with clients, departments, and permissions, as you'll learn later in this chapter.

Setting Up Projects, Areas, and Releases

After you've created your FogBugz users, you'll probably want to set up projects and areas within those projects. Projects and areas form a hierarchy that lets you sort cases in ways that make sense for your organization. Releases add one more dimension to this hierarchy. Each project can have its own set of releases, and you can also share releases between projects.

Creating and Editing Projects

It's possible that your organization is small enough that you're only working on a single project. But more likely, you've got more than one iron in the fire. On a typical software team, you'll set up a project for each individual product that you have under development. This lets you sort cases so that the developers, testers, and managers working on a particular product only have to deal with the cases that concern them.

■**Tip** Don't make the mistake of thinking that projects absolutely must map directly to products. If your requirements are unusual, it may make more sense to brainstorm an alternative arrangement. For example, if your primary business is customizing an off-the-shelf product for a vertical market, and you assign customization to representatives around the country, you may want to set up one project for each geographical region.

If you're an administrator, you can see a list of projects that are already in the system by clicking the Projects link on the Administrative Tools bar. This will open the list shown in Figure 3-4.

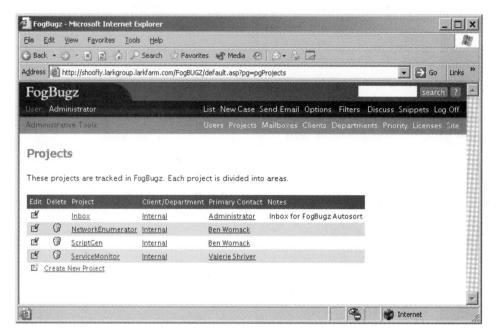

Figure 3-4. *List of projects in FogBugz*

Note You'll see in Figure 3-4 that one of the projects has a note indicating that it's an Inbox. Only e-mail–enabled projects will have such a note, and you can't edit these notes yourself through the FogBugz user interface. See Chapter 5 for more information on e-mail enabling a FogBugz project.

From the project list, you can perform these actions:

- Edit a project by clicking the edit icon or the project name.

- Delete a project by clicking the delete icon.

- View details on the associated client or department by clicking the client or department name (you'll learn more about clients and departments later in this chapter in the section "Setting Up Clients and Departments").

- View details about the project's primary contact by clicking the primary contact's name.

- Create a new project by clicking the icon or text at the bottom of the list.

When you choose to create a new project, FogBugz presents you with the screen shown in Figure 3-5.

To get started, you need to choose a name for the new project. Ordinarily, this should be the name of the product, though you can use any arbitrary string of characters up to 128 characters in length.

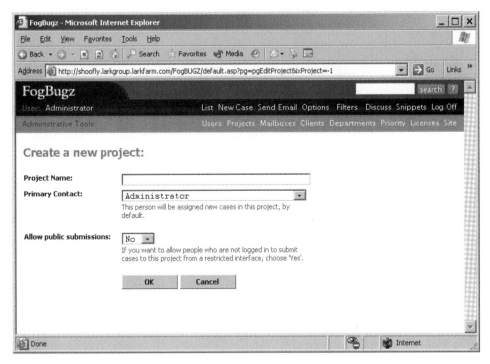

Figure 3-5. *Creating a new project*

■**Tip** Don't include the release number in the project name; you'll set up releases for that. By including multiple releases of the same product in one project, instead of creating a project for each release, you'll make it easier to move cases from one release to another.

You also need to select a FogBugz user to be the primary contact for the new project. The primary contact is the person whom you've designated to look at cases and assign them to the appropriate person to fix. When someone enters a new case, they usually leave it assigned to the primary contact, the default. The primary contact will get e-mail as soon as the case is saved for the first time, so they'll know to look at the case and assign it to the proper person on their team.

■**Tip** If you are working on a large project team, you may want to have several people who help categorize new cases. To do this, you can (assuming you have enough licenses) set up a virtual user account called "Up For Grabs" and make Up For Grabs the owner of the project. You can use as many e-mail addresses as you want for Up For Grabs, separated by commas, so that a group of people receives an e-mail notification whenever there's a new bug in a particular project. Anyone who wants to help sort through new bugs can create a saved filter on "all cases assigned to Up For Grabs," which they check occasionally.

Finally, you can choose whether to allow public submissions to the project. If you do allow public submissions, and your FogBugz server is at a URL that is publicly available, then it's possible to submit cases to the project without being logged in to FogBugz. In most cases, I'd suggest you use the e-mail features of FogBugz to allow anonymous cases and keep your FogBugz server off the Internet instead of allowing direct public submissions, for a little bit of extra security.

Clicking OK on this screen will create the new project and return you to the list of projects. The next step is to click the project name so that you can create areas and releases for the project. Figure 3-6 shows the project editing screen for a brand new project.

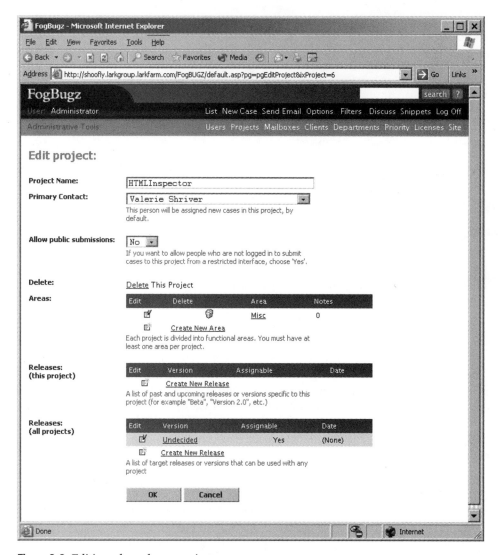

Figure 3-6. *Editing a brand new project*

Creating and Editing Areas

Within each project, you can divide cases into areas. The primary use of areas is to let people find the cases that they'd like to work with by creating filters for a particular area. For example, you might have separate areas for the code and the documentation of your project.

In general, you'll find that the fewer areas you have, the more likely people are to categorize cases correctly into the right area. Think of it this way: if you have 100 areas, everybody who enters a case is going to have to consider each of those 100 areas to decide which area is the best fit. Inevitably, cases will be miscategorized, and the pain of choosing an area may even make people enter fewer cases. If it's easier to jot down a case than enter it into FogBugz, you're going to lose the benefit of bug tracking.

When you first create a project, FogBugz creates a default area for that project named Misc. To create a new area, click the Create New Area link on the project's editing screen. This will open a screen that prompts you for the single piece of information required to define an area: the area's name. Enter a name, click OK, and FogBugz will create the area.

■Tip FogBugz automatically creates special areas to handle spam and unsorted mail in e-mail–enabled projects. You'll be able to identify these areas by notes on the listing of areas. You can't add notes to your own custom areas through the FogBugz user interface.

You can also edit and delete areas from the project editing screen. If you delete an area, cases that were previously assigned to that area remain assigned to that area, but you cannot assign new cases to that area.

For many projects, you'll be able to identify a small set of areas, each of which belongs to a different user. For example, you might end up with Documentation, Setup, and Core as your areas, as well as the default catch-all Misc area. Set up these few areas when you first create the project, and use them to categorize the initial cases as they come in. Then add areas only after careful consideration and only if they are needed for a particular filter that you want to create. For example, if you have a developer concentrating on the Web interface, and they need to see all the bugs related to the Web interface, create an area named Web UI. Don't create more areas than you need for filters, because the more you have, the more likely cases will be misfiled.

Creating and Editing Releases

Another way to categorize cases within a project is by the release of the software. You'll want to have one release in FogBugz for each release of the software that you plan to make. Even when a project is just getting underway, you can probably visualize the first several releases: Alpha, Beta 1, Beta 2, RC1, RC2, 1.0, and 2.0 might make a reasonable initial set. Unless you have an overwhelming number of development and testing resources to call on, you probably need to project your releases into the future. That way, as you're considering bugs and feature requests, you'll have the flexibility available to assign them to future releases. It's a fact of software life that we rarely get everything we want into the first (or second, or third) release of a project.

You'll find two sections for releases on the project editing screen: Releases (This Project) and Releases (All Projects). FogBugz ships with a release called "Undecided" as a default global release (that is, one that's available to all projects). If you don't do anything to create more releases, every project will let you assign cases to the Undecided release, which doesn't have a particular due date. To edit a global release, go into any project's editing screen. Another useful global release is one named ASAP for things that need to be done right away. The ASAP release doesn't exist by default, but as you'll see shortly, it's easy to create one.

To create a new release, click one of the Create New Release links on the project editing screen (which one depends on whether you want the release to be available only in this project or to be available in all projects). This will open the screen shown in Figure 3-7.

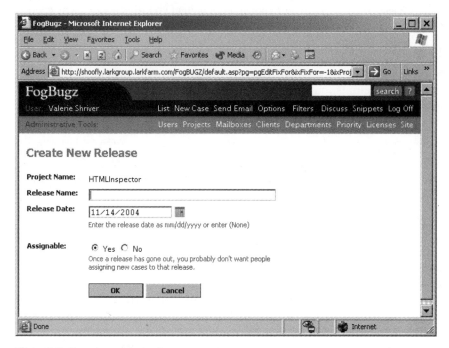

Figure 3-7. *Creating a new release*

To create a release, give it a name (such as "1.0" or "Third beta") and assign it a release date. You can change this date later, but you should try to pick a realistic date in the first place so that people can budget their efforts. The other property you can set for a release is whether it's assignable. After a release has already shipped, it doesn't make any sense to assign new cases to it. You should set the Assignable field of the release to "No" to prevent new cases being assigned to a release that has already shipped. This also makes the list of releases shown when you enter a new case shorter by not showing this release at all.

■**Tip** You can use plain language such as "next month" or "pnext Tuesday" in the Release Date field, and FogBugz will convert the text to an actual date when you tab out of the field. You can also click the calendar icon to choose a date on a calendar.

When you click OK to create a new release, FogBugz will return you to the project editing screen. You can edit the details of a release by clicking the edit icon or the name of the release. Note that you can't delete a release. If you no longer want a release to be available, edit the release and set it to be nonassignable.

The date of a release doesn't necessarily need to be a date. You can also use "(None)" to create a release with no date. But you can't use arbitrary text as the release date. If you want to tie a release to an event rather than a calendar date, set the release date to "(None)" and set the name of the release to the event, for example, "ASAP" or "Never" or "After VC Funding".

All of the assignable releases for a project will show up in the Fix For drop-down list when you enter a new case for that project. By default, new cases will be assigned to the Undecided global release, but whoever reviews new cases should assign them to their proper release quickly. This makes it easier to tell how much of the workload is assigned to each release.

As the date for a release nears, you'll probably want to create a filter to see all of the features and bugs that are assigned to that release.

When a certain release is coming up, you can create a filter to see all the features and bugs that need to be fixed for that release. Figure 3-8 shows how you might create a filter for a particular release. Note that you need to select the project first to see all of the releases for that particular project in the release drop-down list. In this case, the user is also choosing to focus only on active, open cases.

■Note For more information on working with filters, see Chapter 2.

When you fix a bug or implement a new feature, before you resolve the case, double-check that the Fix For setting is correct; that way a filter on a past release can also be used as an historical record of which bugs were fixed in that release, and which new features were implemented for that release.

FogBugz also allows you to create release notes tied to a particular release and to update these release notes as you close cases assigned to the release. I'll discuss release notes in Chapter 4.

Don't confuse releases and versions. When you're entering a new case, you pick the release from a drop-down list, and enter the version as free-form text. The release is when you plan for the bug to be fixed or the feature to be implemented. The version is when you spotted the bug. Typically, you'll have more versions than releases; if you're using an automated build process, you probably have one version per day, or even more.

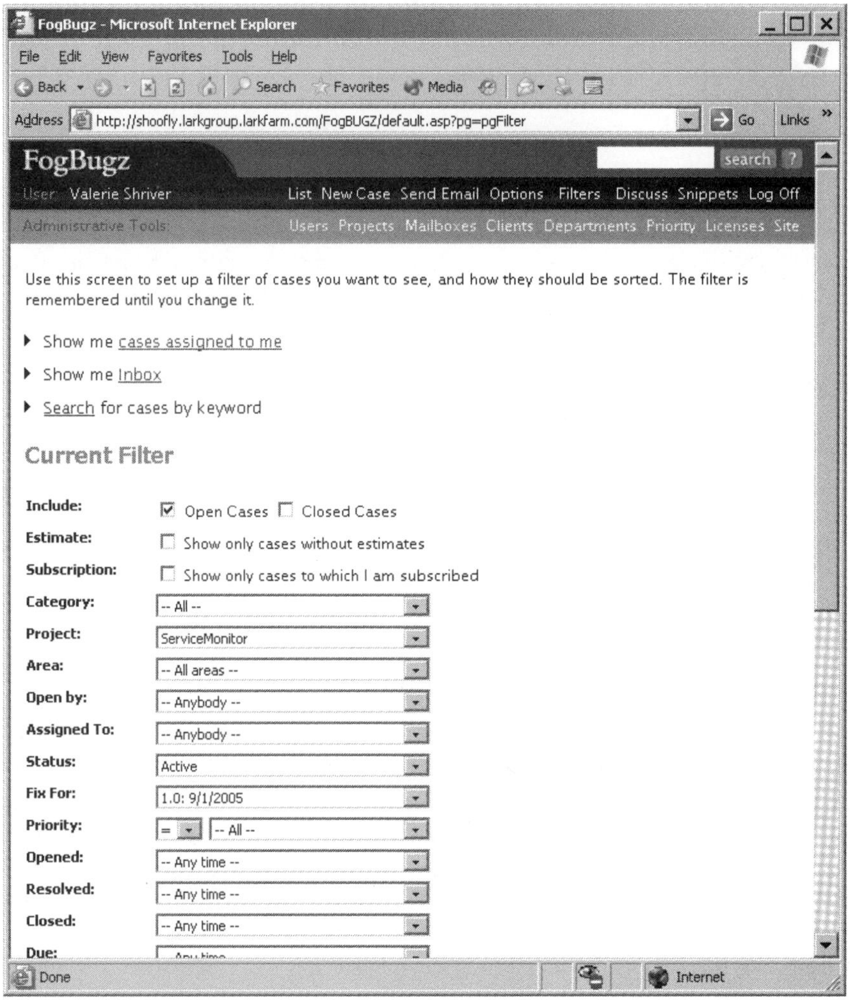

Figure 3-8. *Filtering by release*

Setting Up Clients and Departments

The levels of grouping I've been discussing so far apply to individual cases. But FogBugz offers two optional ways to group your projects as well. These groupings can't be applied to individual cases, but they're still useful in organizing your cases:

- Grouping by client

- Grouping by department

Grouping projects by client is helpful when you work with multiple clients, each of which may have multiple projects. You can also group projects by department, which is helpful when your team is divided into different departments, each of which may work on multiple projects.

■Note Internally, clients and departments are treated in exactly the same way: they're both ways to group projects. Because clients and departments are stored in the same table in the FogBugz database, each project can be assigned to exactly one client or one department, but not both.

FogBugz installs with a default client named Internal and no departments. To use these grouping features, you first need to set up your clients or departments (or both). Log on as an administrator and click the Clients link to get a list of clients, as shown in Figure 3-9.

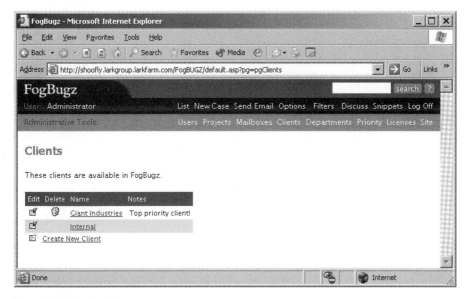

Figure 3-9. *Listing clients*

From the client listing screen, you can

- Click the edit icon or the client name to edit the details of the client.

- Click the Delete icon to delete the client. Note that you cannot delete the default Internal client.

- Create a new client by clicking the Create New Client link.

When you click the Create New Client link, FogBugz will open the screen shown in Figure 3-10.

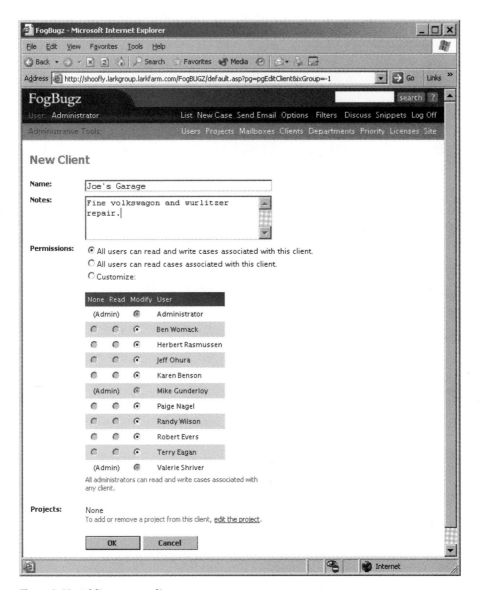

Figure 3-10. *Adding a new client*

To create a client, you need to give the client a name and, optionally, some notes. Then click the OK button to create the client. You can also assign permissions on a user-by-user basis; I'll discuss permissions in the next section of this chapter.

Creating a department works very much like creating a client. There's a department listing page that looks like the client listing page, and a department edit page that looks like the client edit page. In fact, they're pretty much the same pages, with the exception of saying "department" instead of "client" everywhere.

After you've created the clients or departments that you need, edit your projects one by one. As soon as you create any clients or departments, the editing screen for a project will display a new drop-down list that lets you choose the client or department, as shown in Figure 3-11.

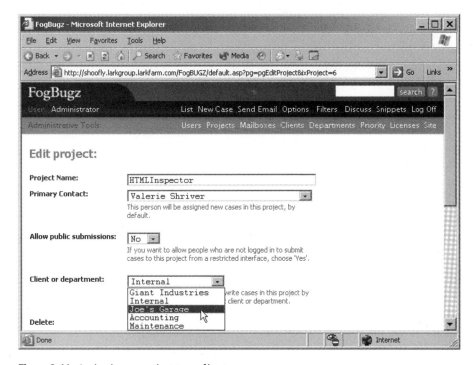

Figure 3-11. *Assigning a project to a client*

There are two main reasons that you'd want to group projects by client or department. First, doing so allows you to create a filter that lists all cases for a certain client or all cases in a certain department that you care about. Second, user access can be granted on a client or departmental level. This means that it's possible to create FogBugz accounts for your clients such that they can only see their own cases. You can also partition departments so that users can only see cases in their own department. I'll cover these techniques next.

Setting Up Permissions

The major reason for setting up clients and departments is to use them for access control. FogBugz allows you to set up permissions (access control) so that only certain users can see or modify certain cases. Before you can start assigning permissions, you need to create at least one client or department.

Typically, you will use FogBugz access control for one of two purposes:

- Hiding clients from each other

- Limiting users to their own department

If you have multiple external clients, you can give them all accounts on your FogBugz database without letting them see each other's cases or even know about each other. When your client logs on to FogBugz, they will only be able to see cases associated with their projects, not with the projects of other clients. They won't even be able to find out about the other clients: they will have no way of seeing cases, users, or projects unless you specifically grant them permission (assuming you set things up correctly, that is).

Similarly, if you are using a single FogBugz installation for multiple departments, you can set things up so that users only have permission to see cases in their own department.

FogBugz will give a particular user permission to access all the cases associated with one or more clients or departments. This means that before you can start assigning permissions, you need to follow the procedures I discussed earlier in the chapter to create clients or departments, and then assign projects to the appropriate client or department.

■**Caution** Permissions are only useful if you require passwords to log on to FogBugz. See Appendix A for details on the password options of FogBugz. If you don't set passwords, anyone can log on as any user, which defeats the purpose of permissions.

Isolating Clients with Permissions

To get a feel for what you can do with permissions, consider a software consulting business working in a vertical market—say, customizing software for window-washing companies. The company employs a number of consultants, each of whom should only be able to see cases related to the clients that they service. To provide faster service, the company also allows personnel from the clients to access their internal FogBugz server through special accounts. Of course, if an employee of a client signs on, they should only be allowed to see their own cases. In fact, if an employee of Highrise Window Washers logs on, the company doesn't even want them to be aware that Plate O'Glass Co. is also a client.

The key to making this work is to set up permissions properly in FogBugz. Whenever FogBugz shows a drop-down list of users, it will not include everyone. It will only list users that you might encounter because you share permission to access some client or department. For example, consultants Alice and Bob are working on the Highrise Window Washers account only, while Mike is working on the Plate O'Glass account only. Normally, Alice and Bob will see each other in the user drop-down list, but they'll never see Mike's name in a drop-down list or in a case, and vice versa. So if you make an account for the president of Highrise Window Washers in your FogBugz database, this name won't show up in drop-down lists when a Plate O'Glass client logs on. This helps keep all the clients happy and secure in the knowledge that you're concentrating all of your efforts on their behalf.

But . . . and this is an important but . . . if you set up any clients who are visible to all users, this protection is lost. For example, if the consulting company has a third client, the local Petting Zoo, and thinks that, heck, the Petting Zoo doesn't have anything confidential, we might as well let everyone in there, they run the risk that a Highrise Window Washers executive and a Plate O'Glass executive will run into each other's names in the user drop-down list, since they share access to the Petting Zoo, and flip out. In summary, if you need to isolate users from one another, you can *never* have any clients that everyone can access.

Isolating Departments with Permissions

In a very large company with lots of departments or teams, where each department may work on several projects, it can be helpful to divide up the projects according to department, even when there's no security reason to do so. This makes it easy to run filters so that the team management can look at all the cases across an entire department. This also works well when the company is large enough that individual developers and testers are 100% dedicated to a particular department.

If you're using permissions to isolate departments, you probably don't have to be as careful about overlapping permissions as you would with clients. Of course, if you ever need to set up a secret internal project, you can do so by creating a department and making sure that the users for that department aren't assigned to any other projects.

Assigning Permissions

Now that you know the theory of assigning permissions in FogBugz, it's time to look at how it works in practice. FogBugz supports three levels of permissions:

- *None*: A given user does not have permission to see or modify cases.

- *Read*: A given user can read cases, but can't modify them in any way.

- *Modify*: A given user can read and modify cases.

  Permissions are set up on a client or department basis, and then applied to all projects assigned to that client or department. When you are editing a client or department in FogBugz, you have three choices. First, you can choose to give everyone full access to the client or department, as shown in Figure 3-12. This is the default. With this setting, you can't change the permissions for individual users.

Figure 3-12. *Giving everyone full access to a client*

The second choice is to give everyone read access to the client or department, as shown in Figure 3-13. In this case, you can control on a user-by-user basis which users can modify cases for the client or department. Administrators, though, will always have modify access.

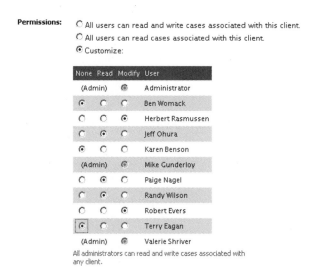

Figure 3-13. *Giving everyone read access to a client*

Finally, you can choose to customize access to the client or department. In this case, you can choose on a user-by-user basis whether to assign none, read, or modify access. Administrators still get modify access automatically, as shown in Figure 3-14.

Permissions: ○ All users can read and write cases associated with this client.
○ All users can read cases associated with this client.
◉ Customize:

None	Read	Modify	User
(Admin)		◉	Administrator
◉	○	○	Ben Womack
○	○	◉	Herbert Rasmussen
○	◉	○	Jeff Ohura
◉	○	○	Karen Benson
(Admin)		◉	Mike Gunderloy
○	◉	○	Paige Nagel
○	◉	○	Randy Wilson
○	○	◉	Robert Evers
◉	○	○	Terry Eagan
(Admin)		◉	Valerie Shriver

All administrators can read and write cases associated with any client.

Figure 3-14. *Assigning custom permissions for a client*

It's important to understand the consequences of your choices in editing this section of clients and departments. If you choose option #1 or #2 for any client or department, you will not be able to completely segregate groups of users from each other, because they can meet each other in that client or department. The net effect is that if you want to use permissions to keep users separated and hidden from one another, you need to set up custom permissions for every single client and department.

■**Caution** Don't forget to set custom permissions on the default Internal client when you're setting up a custom permissions scheme.

Anyone who is configured as a FogBugz administrator will always have permission to read, write, and modify any case, anywhere. A corollary of this is that the administrators can see all of the other users, and all users can see the administrators.

To sum up, there are four things you need to do when setting up a custom permissions scheme in FogBugz:

- Use the Site Options screen to ensure that FogBugz is configured to require passwords to log on.

- Create the appropriate clients or departments.

- Edit the clients or departments to assign user permissions appropriately.

- Assign each project to the appropriate client or department.

Setting Up Priorities

Every case in the system is given a priority from 1 to 7, where 1 is the highest priority and 7 is the lowest. Developers and testers can (and should!) use these priorities to help them focus on the things that are most important to fix. Of course, you can't set a firm rule that you need to always work in priority order (for example, a priority 3 bug that needs to be fixed by beta 1 probably needs attention before a priority 1 bug that needs to be fixed by the final release, especially if beta 1 is scheduled to ship tomorrow), but priorities act as a good starting point for ordering your work.

FogBugz doesn't let you change the number of priority levels, but you can rename the text labels given to priority 1 through 7 to suit your preferences. To do so, log on as an administrator and click the Priority link in the Administrative Tools bar. Figure 3-15 shows the default labels for the seven priorities.

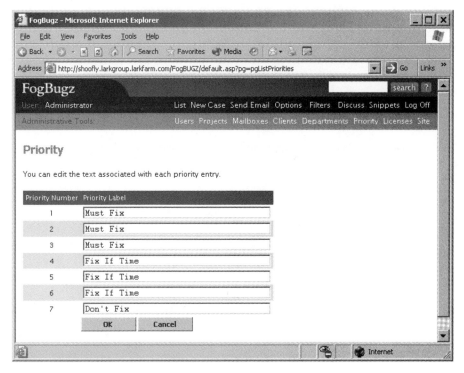

Figure 3-15. *Modifying the labels for priorities*

To change the priority labels, type in your new text and then click OK. As you can see, the default scheme uses the same label for several different priorities. If your users find this confusing ("Why are some Must Fix items more important than others?"), you might like to move to a scheme such as this where each priority has a distinctive label:

1. Drop everything and fix.

2. A customer is waiting for this.

3. Very important.

4. Important.

5. Less important—fix before playing Minesweeper.

6. Probably won't fix but worth remembering.

7. Not worth wasting time on.

Setting Up Versions and Computers

When someone reports a bug, you might find it helpful to know what version of the software they saw the bug in. This might be a shipping version (e.g., "2.0 with service pack 2") or it may be a development version ("the build that Harry gave me on 9/5/06"). Similarly, you might like some details about the computer where the bug was spotted ("an old Pentium II box we use in the lab").

These two pieces of information aren't amenable to capturing in simple lists (like the lists of priorities or areas). There are probably a lot more versions than releases; many programming shops have builds every day, and it is helpful in reporting a bug to indicate exactly which build it was found in. Similarly, you probably can't enumerate all of the computers that your testers might be using. That's why these two pieces of information are better captured in free-form text.

FogBugz includes two plain text fields that can be used to track versions and computers (or, for that matter, any other two pieces of information). By default, these fields are hidden to simplify entering cases. If you're an administrator, you can turn these fields on and customize them by clicking the Site link in the Administrative Links toolbar. Figure 3-16 shows the part of the Site Configuration screen where you can customize these fields.

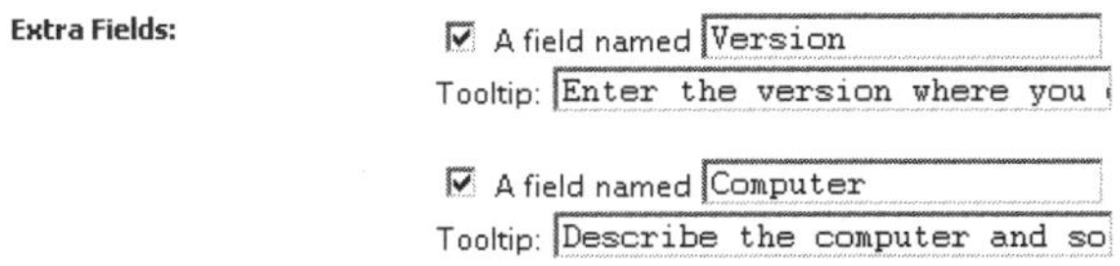

Extra Fields:

☑ A field named `Version`
Tooltip: `Enter the version where you `

☑ A field named `Computer`
Tooltip: `Describe the computer and so`

Figure 3-16. *Customizing the free text fields*

To turn either or both of these fields on, check the checkbox. You can also customize both the display name of the field and the longer explanation that FogBugz gives as a tooltip.

When you enter a new case, the default version and computer will be the same as the last case you entered; this way, if you are testing a particular version of code on a particular computer and you find lots of bugs, you don't have to keep reentering the version and computer details. Of course, this memory facility works even if you've renamed the fields to hold other information.

Customizing Your Working Schedule

FogBugz has an internal notion of when your team should be at work. This working schedule is used for two purposes. First, it calculates an automatic due date for incoming e-mail, based on the e-mail policies you've set up. Suppose, for example, your policy is to respond to all e-mail within 12 hours. If an e-mail comes in at 3 p.m. Friday, and you only work 9 a.m. until 6 p.m. on weekdays, and not at all on weekends, FogBugz is smart enough to set the due date to 9 a.m. on Tuesday. The second use for the working schedule is to convert between hours and days when storing estimates for a case.

Administrators can customize the working schedule to fit their company's needs. To do so, log on as an administrator and click the Site link in the Administrative Tools bar. Scroll down on the site configuration page and click the Working Schedule link to open the Working Schedule screen, shown in Figure 3-17.

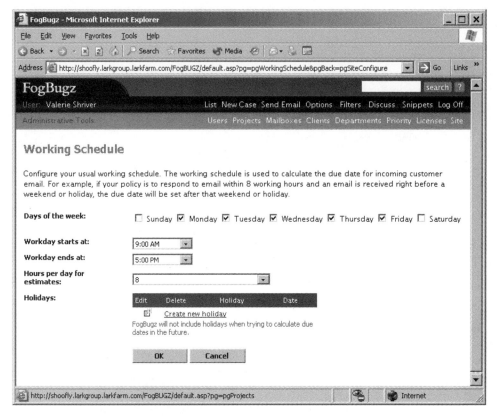

Figure 3-17. *Customizing the working schedule*

You can set up several things on this screen:

- Choose which days of the week your team works by checking the boxes for those days.

- Choose the starting and ending time for workdays. This setting applies to all of the days that you check; you can't have separate hours for weekends.

- Choose how many hours equal one day when you're entering or adjusting the estimated time to close a case.

- Specify holiday dates that are not counted as working dates at all. To enter a holiday, click the Create New Holiday link, which opens the screen shown in Figure 3-18.

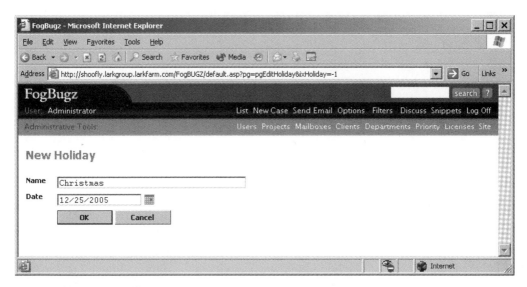

Figure 3-18. *Creating a holiday*

■**Note** FogBugz doesn't have any notion of a repeating holiday. If you want to give your employees every Christmas off, you'll need to remember to enter the date each year.

Applying Bulk Actions to Cases

Sometimes you'll want to operate on cases in bulk. For example, suppose you've just reviewed all of the cases for a particular product and realized that there are a substantial number related to the setup and installation of the product. You decide to create a new area named Setup and then assign the setup-related cases to this area. But going through each case a second time to change its area would be tedious. That's where the bulk-editing capabilities of FogBugz come in handy. You can do nearly anything with a group of cases that you can do with a single case.

To start, build a filter that includes all of the cases that you're interested in, and then go to the list page. At the far left of the page, you'll see a set of checkboxes, as shown in Figure 3-19.

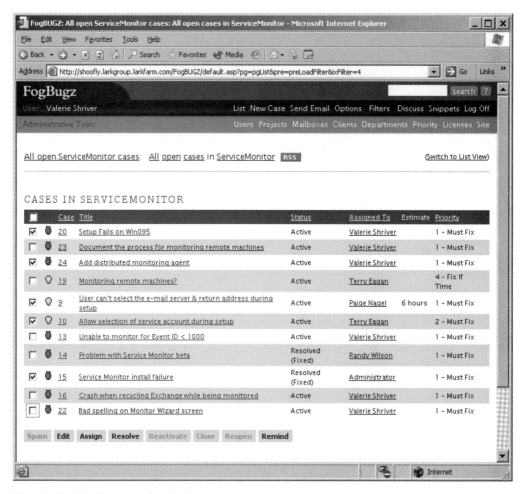

Figure 3-19. *Selecting cases for a bulk action*

Check the boxes next to the cases that you're interested in, and then click one of the action buttons at the bottom of the list. In this case, you're interested in editing the selected cases, so click the Edit button. This will open the bulk editing screen shown in Figure 3-20.

■**Tip** Clicking the checkbox in the column header selects or unselects all the bugs on the page.

■**Tip** To select any range of consecutive bugs, check the first box, then hold down the Shift key and check the last box.

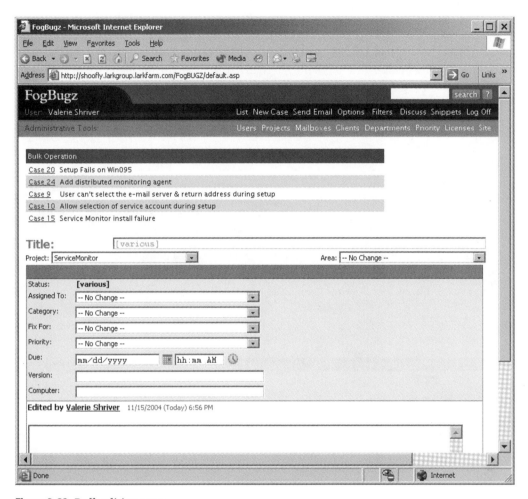

Figure 3-20. *Bulk editing cases*

The bulk editing screen looks very much like the normal case editing screen, but there are several differences:

- The top of the screen lists all of the cases that will be affected by the editing operation.

- You can't change the title field (because it wouldn't make sense to assign the same title to a whole group of cases).

- The various dropdown lists include "-- No Change --" as a choice. This allows you to let cases retain their own individual information.

- The page doesn't display the history of each case, though it does let you enter notes related to this edit.

Make any changes you like (in this case, selecting Setup as the area) and then click OK to apply the change to all of the selected cases. FogBugz will make the change and then show you a confirming screen, similar to the one in Figure 3-21. If you like, you can use the action buttons to perform further bulk operations here. Alternatively, you can use the menu bar to go back to the original list of cases.

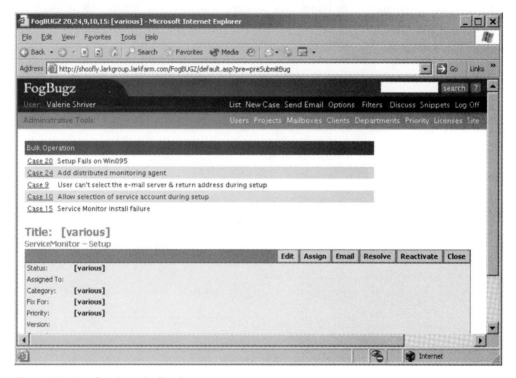

Figure 3-21. *Confirming a bulk edit*

Depending on the cases that you select from the original list, you can perform a variety of bulk operations:

- If the cases are all in an e-mail inbox project, you can dismiss them as spam.

- You can edit the details of the cases, as you've already seen.

- You can assign the cases to a specific user.

- If all of the cases are open, you can resolve them.

- If all of the cases are resolved, you can reactivate them or close them.

- If all of the cases are closed, you can reopen them.

- You can send a reminder about the cases.

Figure 3-22 shows the screen that comes up when you choose to send a reminder about multiple cases. FogBugz constructs an e-mail message listing the cases in question together with their links. By default, the message will come from the user who sets up the reminder and go to all of the users who are currently assigned any of the cases. You can edit any of these fields, of course, together with the subject of the e-mail.

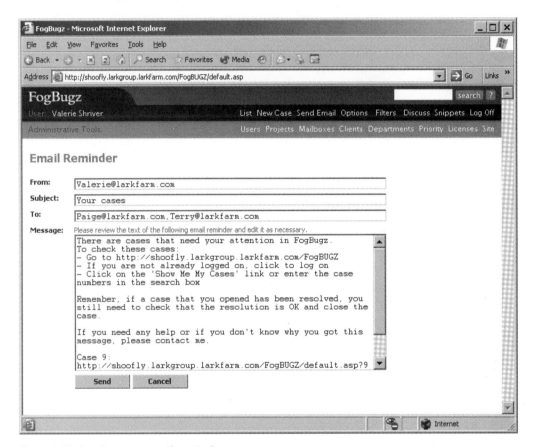

Figure 3-22. *Sending an e-mail reminder*

Summary

In this chapter, you've learned about many of the things that you need to set up to customize FogBugz for your own use. You saw how the FogBugz administrator can create projects and areas, users, clients, departments, and so on. You learned about the FogBugz permission system and saw how you can use the bulk editing feature of FogBugz to save time.

So far, though, you've been focused exclusively on individual cases and what you can do with them. In the next chapter, I'll pull back and look at some of the management features that FogBugz offers to keep a project on track.

■ ■ ■

CHAPTER 4

Getting the Big Picture

You've seen how to use FogBugz to enter and work with cases from the developer's point of view. You've also learned how to perform a variety of administrative tasks with FogBugz to make it perfect for your own organization. Now it's time to move on to another aspect of project management with FogBugz: the actual management part of the job. FogBugz includes several features to help you keep your development running smoothly and on time:

- Time estimates

- Due dates

- Escalation reports

- E-mail and RSS notifications

- Case resolutions

- Release notes

- Custom reports

In this chapter, I'll show you how to effectively use these features of FogBugz. I'll also show you how you can use the data contained in the FogBugz database to create your own customized management reports.

Tracking Estimates

When you're focusing in on a case or a group of cases, one key piece of information is how long they're going to take to resolve. Without this information, there's no way to judge whether a particular developer is overloaded or coasting. Just counting the number of open cases won't do it; depending on who entered the case and what it covers, a case might take 15 minutes or 15 days to resolve. Fortunately, FogBugz lets you provide detailed estimates for how long a case will take to resolve in hours or days, and how much time has already been spent on it.

Maintaining a Case Estimate

To help make estimates of when a case or an entire project will be complete, FogBugz lets you enter an estimate for any case. An estimate can be given in days or hours (or both). To enter an estimate, you use d for days and h for hours; both parts are optional. For example, all of these are acceptable estimates:

- .25h (15 minutes)

- 4h (4 hours)

- 15h (15 hours; FogBugz will convert this to the equivalent in days and hours when you save the case.)

- 2d (2 days)

- 1d6h (1 day and 6 hours)

- 1.5d (1½ days; FogBugz will convert this to the equivalent in days and hours when you save the case.)

■**Note** By default, FogBugz assumes that the working day is 8 hours long, so that 1.5d is converted to 1d4h. Administrators can adjust the length of the working day, and FogBugz will change the conversion accordingly. For example, if you force your workers to do mandatory overtime and work 10 hours a day, 15h will convert to 1d5h. On the other hand, if your team only comes in for half days and works an average of 4 hours, 15h becomes 3d3h. For details on adjusting working hours, see Chapter 3.

For cases that can be resolved quickly, you can enter less than an hour by using fractional hours: .5h for 30 minutes, .25h for 15 minutes, even 0.1h for 6 minutes. The only estimate that you can't enter is 0h, because that would be indistinguishable from not having entered an estimate at all. Anyhow, you can't resolve a case in no time, no matter how efficient you are!

If you ever change an estimate, the original estimate is shown above the current estimate. This is useful if you want to go back to your old bugs and see how good a job you've done estimating in the past, so you can learn to estimate better in the future. Once you enter a nonzero estimate for a case, FogBugz also allows you to enter the elapsed time. FogBugz will automatically calculate the remaining time based on the current estimate and the elapsed time. For features whose work spans several days, at the end of every day's work, you can reenter your current best-guess estimate and the amount of time spent so far. This helps ensure that the total time estimated in the system is as accurate as it can be.

Let's look at this process in practice with an actual case. Figure 4-1 shows the initial state of a case representing a new feature that needs to be added to the Service Monitor application.

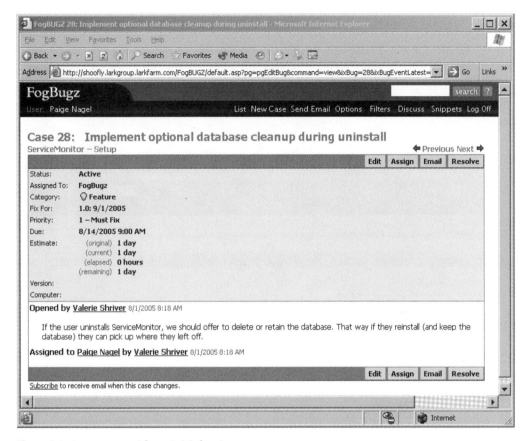

Figure 4-1. *A new case with an initial estimate*

In Figure 4-1, Paige has logged on to her account to discover that her manager, Valerie, entered a new case and assigned it to Paige. Because Valerie entered an initial estimate when she created the case, FogBugz shows four values in the Estimate section of the case:

- The original estimate

- The current estimate

- The actual elapsed time

- The estimated time remaining

■Tip Don't enter an estimate when you create a case unless you think you can be reasonably accurate. It's easy to search for cases with no estimate (by setting up a filter) but impossible to search for cases with inaccurate estimates. Use your judgment; if you're a manager parceling out features based on a detailed spec, you probably have a good idea of how long the work will take, but if you're a tester who finds a mysterious bug, it's tough to know what will be involved in fixing it.

Paige has some other cases on her plate that are due sooner, but she doesn't want this one to creep up on her by surprise. So she blocks out an hour of her day to investigate the problem. At the end of that time, she's convinced that the feature can be implemented, but that it will require major changes to the scripting in the setup project. At the end of her work day, Paige edits the case as shown in Figure 4-2.

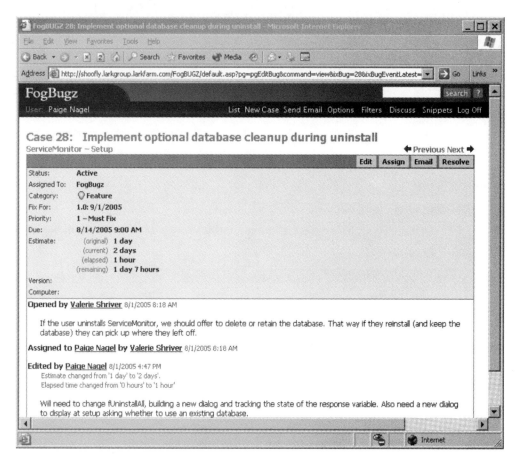

Figure 4-2. *A case with some work and an updated estimate*

■**Tip** An open case makes an excellent place to keep notes to yourself about what needs to be done to close the case.

A few days later, Paige gets time to actually work on the new feature. She puts on her headphones, cranks up the music, and gets into the zone. Miraculously, no one calls an emergency meeting and the corporate e-mail server is down for most of the day, minimizing interruptions. At the end of the day, she thinks she has only another hour of work left, so she edits the case again. Figure 4-3 shows the newly updated case.

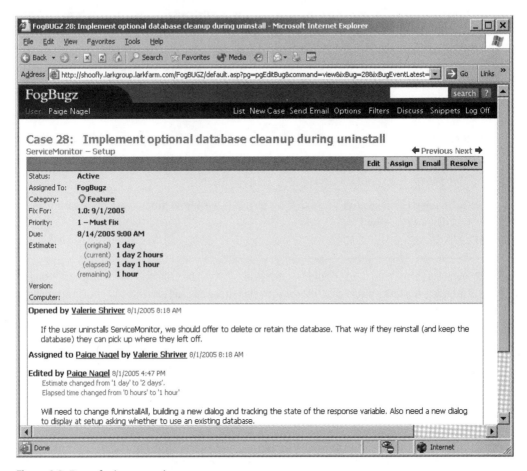

Figure 4-3. *Reupdating an estimate*

As you work on a case, the elapsed time and the current estimate should converge to the same number. Then, when you mark the case resolved, you should set the final estimate and the elapsed time to the actual time worked. Of course, if the case needs to be reopened later, you'll find yourself increasing the estimate once again.

Using Estimates to Manage Workload

Estimates are also very useful if you're trying to keep track of the total time left to resolve a group of cases. At the bottom of any list of cases, FogBugz will always calculate a summary of the estimated remaining time for all cases shown in that particular list. If you are careful to maintain estimates and elapsed time as you go along, you can use these summaries to get a good approximation of how much work is left for any set of cases. There are many uses for such a list, depending on which filter you use to construct the list. For example:

- If you're a manager, you can filter for unresolved cases in a particular release to get an estimate of how much work remains to be done to ship that release.

- If you're a manager, you can filter for unresolved cases assigned to particular developers to tell who's overloaded and who's not.

- If you're a developer, you can look at your own cases to see just how overloaded you are.

- If you're a tester, you can see how good a job you're doing at keeping the developers overloaded.

- If you need to make cuts, you can filter by area to see how much work eliminating a particular area would save.

▓**Tip** Summing estimates is most useful when every case that can be estimated has an estimate. Using filters, it is easy to search for all the bugs without estimates so you can add estimates (or ask the appropriate developer to add estimates).

Figure 4-4 shows how FogBugz presents an estimate with a list of cases. Note the summary at the bottom of the page; it includes the total estimated amount of time remaining, as well as the number of cases with no estimate. You can also see the estimates for individual cases by referring to the detailed list.

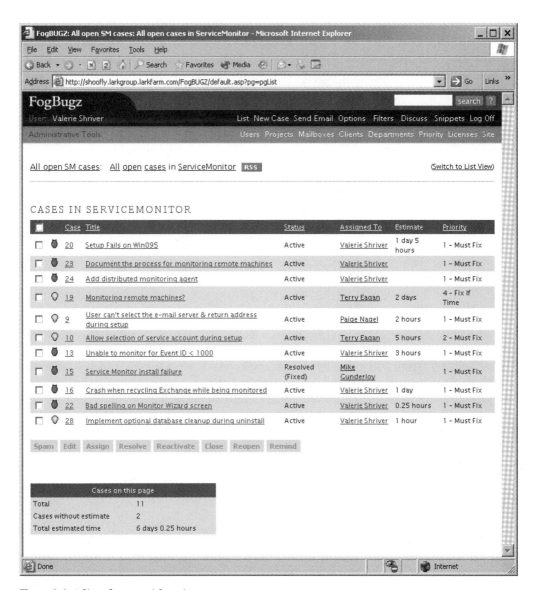

Figure 4-4. *A list of cases with estimates*

The Art of Estimating

If we could assign perfectly accurate estimates to the time needed to fix bugs and implement features as soon as we knew about them, keeping a software project on track would be much simpler. Alas, in the real world it doesn't work that way. Initial estimates are frequently wrong and need to be revised as work progresses. In fact, as a profession, we're so bad at estimating (especially on large projects) that many software projects never get finished at all. Instead they're cancelled amidst a general atmosphere of slipping schedules and rising costs.

The good news is that there are ways to improve your estimating ability. If you consciously practice and put thought into making good estimates, you can get better at it. Although estimating will always remain an art rather than a science, here are some tips that you can use to improve your estimates:

- When entering cases (especially features), strive to make them cover as little as possible. The smaller the task, the better you'll be able to estimate it. For example, "add Web integration" is hopelessly broad, and any estimate the developer makes will probably be wildly inaccurate. "Implement uploading log files via FTP" is a much more easily estimated task. Some people call these fine-grained tasks inch-pebbles to indicate that they're much smaller than milestones.

- While a manager may enter an original estimate based on a project plan, the actual estimate must be owned by the developer who's actually doing the work. You can't get a 10-hour feature done in 5 hours simply by chopping the estimate in half.

- Keep all the work that has to be done in a single system (such as FogBugz!). If there's a place to estimate every task, developers will be less likely to pad estimates to include time for "off the books" work. When you run into a new task that's not on the project, take the time to enter a case for it.

- After you've been entering estimates for a while, take the time to review the original and final estimates on your own closed cases to look for patterns. If you consistently have to add 50% to your original estimate, for example, you should adjust your original estimates by 50% when you make them. Almost every developer is too optimistic when they start estimating the time that it will take to fix a bug or implement a feature.

- Keep the schedule up to date. You should update the current estimate and elapsed time on all of your open cases once a day in most cases. These continuous small course corrections will help you zero in on accurate estimates.

- If one developer's estimates are wildly inaccurate, have them work with an "estimating mentor" in developing estimates for new cases.

- Don't use estimates to hide a disaster. If you're falling behind, it can be tempting to reduce the estimates of the work remaining on your plate so that your manager doesn't get worried. Perhaps you think you'll catch up by working extra hard. You won't. If there's a problem, it needs to be out in the open where the whole team can solve it, if necessary by reassigning features to other developers or even cutting them. Think of it this way: would you rather look slow but honest six weeks before the beta, or be the person who prevents the beta from going out on time when your poor estimates finally become obvious the week before it's due to ship?

- Don't gold-plate your estimates. If you build in excess time so that you can surf the Web, call your broker, and sleep late, your manager will eventually notice just by looking at the number of features you implement compared to the rest of the team. It's better to estimate as accurately as you can and ask for slack time when you need it.

■**Note** For a more detailed look at the entire project planning process, see Joel Spolsky's essay "Painless Software Schedules," reprinted in *Joel on Software* (Apress, 2004).

Using Due Dates

You can assign any case within FogBugz a due date. In most cases you won't want developers to be assigning their own due dates. Instead, plan on having a manager review each case and decide when it must be finished (this is one good reason to keep your project manager as the default user for the project, so that they get to see new cases first). FogBugz allows a flexible syntax for entering due dates. For example, all of these are valid due dates:

- Today

- Tomorrow

- The day after tomorrow

- In 3 days

- In 1 week

- Tuesday

- Next Friday

- March 1

- 12/30 (or 30.12 outside the USA)

- 12/30/2006 (or 30.12.2006 outside the USA)

- June

In every case, FogBugz will replace the due date with an actual date and time when you leave the data entry textbox.

In addition to entering due dates by hand, you can also set up FogBugz to automatically calculate and enter due dates for one particular class of cases: cases submitted via e-mail. That's because these cases are most likely to be submitted directly by your customers, and so will require attention in a reasonable period of time. If you make this time short enough, you can even make it a marketing point for your company: "We respond to all customer inquiries within one working day!"

To configure automatic due dates, you need to edit the properties of the mailbox that receives the cases (remember, only administrators can edit mailbox properties). Scroll down the mailbox settings page until you find the Due section. By default, as shown in Figure 4-5, the system doesn't automatically assign due dates to incoming mail. This leaves you free to manage due dates for these cases manually, just as you do any other due dates.

Figure 4-5. *A mailbox without an automatic due date*

To have FogBugz calculate a due date for you, click the Automatic option button in the Due Date section. Then choose a unit of time. Figure 4-6 shows setting a 6-hour response time for incoming e-mails to this particular mailbox.

Figure 4-6. *A mailbox with an automatic due date*

You can select from four different units of time:

- Hours

- Working Hours

- Days

- Working Days

The difference is that Hours and Days are absolute time, while Working Hours and Working Days take into account your organization's schedule. For example, suppose that your working hours are 9 a.m. to 6 p.m., Monday through Friday, with weekends off. If a bug comes in at 4 p.m. on Friday afternoon, here's when it would be due under various scenarios:

- With a 4-hour response time, it would be due at 8 p.m. that same Friday.

- With a 4–working-hour response time, it would be due at 11 a.m. the following Monday.

- With a 2-day response time, it would be due at 4 p.m. on Sunday.

- With a 2–working-day response time, it would be due at 4 p.m. on the following Tuesday.

■**Note** Administrators can follow the link that says "Determine Working Schedule and Holidays" to change the hours that are considered working hours. You can set up the days of the week when you work and the hours of each day when you work, and you can provide a list of holidays when you don't work at all. See Chapter 3 for more details on configuring the working schedule.

■**Tip** Even if you set a day or time as outside working hours, you can always manually force a case to be due at that time.

Escalation Reports

Escalation reports work in conjunction with due dates to help you keep track of cases that may need a little extra attention. Anyone can sign up to receive escalation reports via e-mail by checking the appropriate box on their user options screen, as shown in Figure 4-7.

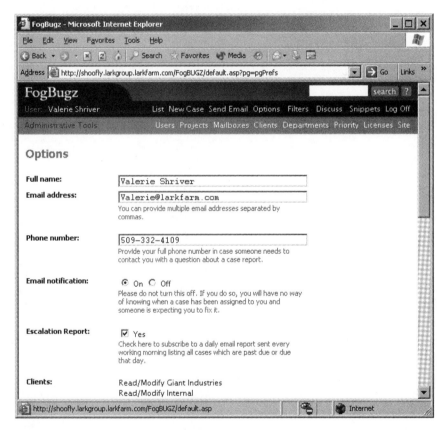

Figure 4-7. *Signing up to receive escalation reports*

An escalation report is sent early every morning via e-mail to each user who is signed up to receive escalation reports. Figure 4-8 shows the format of the e-mail.

FogBugz Escalation Report

fogbugz@example.com

To: Mike Gunderloy

The following cases are past due as of Tuesday, July 12, 2005:

Case 23 - "Document the process for monitoring remote machines"
Case 24 - "Add distributed monitoring agent"

The following cases are due today, Tuesday, July 12, 2005:

Case 27 - "Setup not working on Windows 2003"

For more details, go to
http://shoofly.larkgroup.larkfarm.com/FogBUGZ/default.asp?
pre=preSaveFilterDueToday&pg=pgList

To unsubscribe from this report, go to
http://shoofly.larkgroup.larkfarm.com/FogBUGZ/default.asp?pg=pgPrefs

---

Figure 4-8. *Daily escalation report e-mail*

■**Note** This e-mail comes from the notification return address that the administrator can customize in the site settings. This should be an invalid e-mail address, so that any replies that the user accidentally sends to the address just bounce. Example.com, the domain used in Figure 4-8, is one that's set aside by the Internet authorities for fictitious addresses.

If the user clicks the link in the escalation report e-mail, they'll be taken to their FogBugz account with a filter that lists all cases that are either overdue or will become due that day. Figure 4-9 shows how this list might look.

■**Tip** Even though the filter says it's for open cases due today, it in fact also picks up cases that are overdue today.

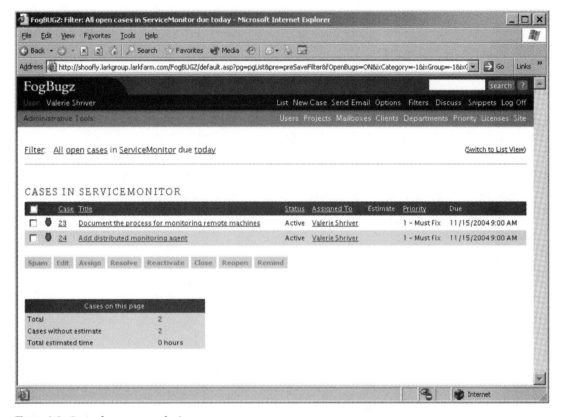

Figure 4-9. *Cases from an escalation report*

You can't easily customize the timescale that the escalation report uses. But you can generate your own filters that let you see cases before they creep up on you. For example, you can set up a filter to list bugs that are going to be due sometime in the future and sort that filter by due date. If you want a two-week view, you can set up a filter listing all cases due in the next two weeks, in order by due date, and check that filter regularly.

Managing E-Mail and RSS Notifications

Filters and reports are good for keeping track of cases when you've got time to sit down and work with FogBugz in your browser. But wouldn't it be nice if FogBugz would actively notify you when a case you're interested in changes? It can! Depending on your needs, you may find e-mail or Really Simple Syndication (RSS) to be a better notification medium.

Using E-Mail Notifications

If you want to make sure you know when someone updates a particular case, e-mail notification is the way to go. At the bottom of each case you'll find a hyperlink to subscribe to the case, as shown in Figure 4-10.

Figure 4-10. *Subscribing to a case*

Click this link (it will then change to read "Unsubscribe") to subscribe to the case. Now, whenever anyone makes a change to the case, FogBugz will send you e-mail to tell you about the change. Figure 4-11 shows a sample notification e-mail.

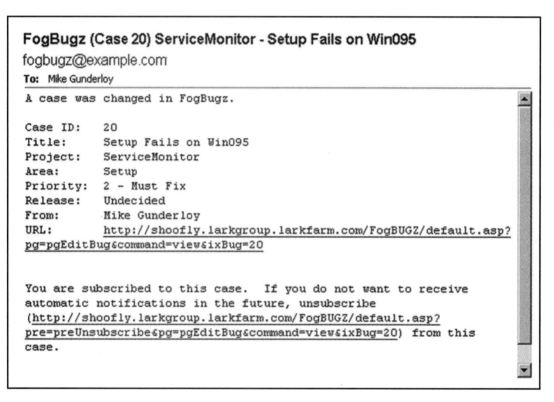

Figure 4-11. *Notification e-mail from FogBugz*

The e-mail contains the essential information to help you remember the case—but it doesn't show the actual change that caused the e-mail to be sent. If you need that level of detail, you need to click the hyperlink to open the case in your browser.

Using RSS Feeds

If you want to track all cases retrieved by a particular filter, you should look at the RSS notification feature of FogBugz. FogBugz publishes RSS feeds, allowing you to use any RSS aggregator to receive notifications, so you can keep up to date on changes to your filter without opening your Web browser. The RSS produced by FogBugz is RSS version 2.0, so any modern aggregator should be able to display it with no problem.

FogBugz creates an RSS feed automatically whenever you save a filter. For the RSS link, go into the Saved Filters screen. You will see a little RSS link at the far right of every saved filter, as shown in Figure 4-12. Copy the link location into your favorite RSS aggregator (following the instructions for that aggregator) and you're ready to go.

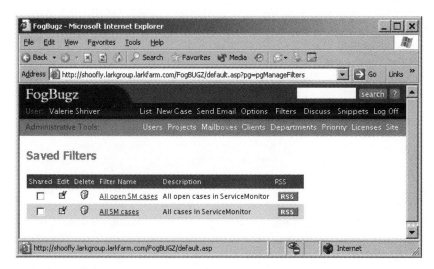

Figure 4-12. *A list of filters with RSS links*

When you subscribe to a filter, your RSS reader will pick up changes to every case covered by the filter. The individual RSS items contain the basic information needed to identify the cases:

- Case number
- URL for further information
- Project
- Area
- Title
- Priority
- Assigned to
- Status
- Current estimate

The RSS items include hyperlinks directly to the case and to the user to whom the case is assigned.

■**Note** Some RSS readers may not support cookies, making it impossible for them to keep you logged on to FogBugz if you're using password security. To work around this problem, you will need to append your user name and password to the end of your feed link manually, according to this pattern: (FogBugz-generated RSS link)&sEmail=*email*&sPassword=*password*.

You can also subscribe to a single bug using RSS, which will notify you as that bug changes. Simply enter the URL of the bug itself in your RSS aggregator, which will automatically discover the URL of the RSS link for that bug. The URL of bug number 1234 is http://fogbugz/?1234, where fogbugz is your main FogBugz URL.

UNDERSTANDING RSS

RSS is an acronym that has stood for several things, depending on who's doing the explaining. I like "Really Simple Syndication" as the expansion, personally. If you don't know about RSS, you're missing out on a major way to get useful information. RSS is a way for a Web site or other information provider to stuff headlines or stories into an XML file with a simple format. Thus, an individual RSS file consists of multiple RSS items. In a FogBugz RSS feed, each case corresponds to an RSS item.

There are dozens of applications out there (generically called "RSS aggregators") that can monitor these files for changes and show you new headlines as they come out. I'm partial to an Outlook-based aggregator called News-Gator (http://www.newsgator.com/). Other popular aggregators include Syndirella (http://www.yole.ru/projects/syndirella/), SharpReader (http://www.hutteman.com/weblog/2003/04/06.html#000056), RSS Bandit (http://www.gotdotnet.com/Community/Workspaces/Workspace.aspx?id=cb8d3173-9f65-46fe-bf17-122e3703bb00), NewzCrawler (http://www.newzcrawler.com/), and FeedReader (http://www.feedreader.com/). For a much more extensive list of RSS aggregators and other RSS tools, refer to http://www.syndic8.com/documents/products/.

Most aggregators work on a "set it and forget it" theory: you tell them how often to look at the RSS feeds (I usually go for once an hour), and when you have time, you read the headlines (in the case of items from FogBugz, the case titles) and decide whether to click through to look at the actual items. It doesn't sound like such a huge advance, but compared with surfing around to dozens of sites to find the items you want to read, RSS is a big improvement. Most people find that they can keep tabs on considerably more information with RSS than with surfing around, and find it easier to home in on the stories that interest them. RSS got its first real burst of popularity from weblogs, but it's now being used by everyone from major media outlets like the BBC and the *New York Times* to technology companies. Microsoft, Sun, Oracle, and IBM are all providing part of their developer-oriented content via RSS these days.

Resolving Cases

As you know, every case in FogBugz needs to be ultimately resolved in some fashion before it can be closed. FogBugz provides 13 different statuses that can be used to close a case (though not all of them apply to every type of case). Any case in the system can be resolved using one of these statuses:

- Duplicate

- By Design

Any bug can be resolved using one of these statuses:

- Fixed

- Not Reproducible

- Postponed

- Won't Fix

Any feature can be resolved using one of these statuses:

- Implemented

- Won't Implement

- Already Exists

Any inquiry can be resolved using one of these statuses:

- Responded

- Won't Respond

- SPAM

- Waiting For Info

▨Tip If you want to resolve a case with a status for another type of case, just change the type when you resolve the case. For example, to close an inquiry as Won't Fix, change the case to a bug before you resolve it.

It's worth understanding, as a team, how each of these statuses will be used. Here are some guidelines that you can start from in determining those common meanings.

Duplicate

Particularly if you've got a product out for active beta testing, you might find the same bug reported two, three, or even more times. When you spot this situation, resolve the extra bugs as duplicates. This will link all of the duplicate bugs together, so you can trace from any of the duplicate bugs back to the bug that you ultimately resolve as fixed. Note that duplicate bugs don't have to describe exactly the same symptoms; as long as a single underlying code change closes all the bugs, they're all duplicates.

By Design

At times, you may get a bug report that describes exactly the way that you think the program should work—in other words, a bug that isn't a bug. For example, an e-mail program could be set up to automatically send forged nondelivery reports to a spam folder. A user who wasn't expecting this might report the action as a bug. In that case, By Design would be the most appropriate way to close the bug. Be careful when using this resolution, though; if something works as you designed, but not as end users expect, it might be time to change your design. Alternatively, you might make a note to explicitly spell out this bit of design in the application's documentation.

Fixed

Sometimes, the best way to resolve a bug is to fix it. In fact, if testers are doing their job well, this will probably be the most common bug resolution in the system.

Not Reproducible

Testers are not infallible, and sometimes you'll get bugs that you simply can't reproduce on your system. Resolve such bugs as not reproducible. Good testers will treat this resolution as a request for more information rather than as an insult, and you may well get the same bug back with additional explanation that makes it possible for you to reproduce the bug. When you're thinking of resolving a bug as not reproducible, try to figure out how the tester could have seen such a thing happen. Is it something that you fixed in a more recent build? Is it an artifact of a particular data file that you don't have? "It works on my machine" is a very unsatisfying explanation for resolving a bug as not reproducible, because, as every tester knows, you're not going to ship your machine to the customer. Leaping to the conclusion that a bug is not reproducible may get it off your desk briefly, but it may also get you dragged down to the test lab to see the bug actually happen.

Resolving a bug as not reproducible is also a common shorthand by developers to say that the tester's bug report is missing repro steps. If a bug is returned to you as not reproducible, that does *not* mean that the bug is fixed or gone, it just means that the developer didn't have enough information to reproduce it. Don't be timid and say, "Oh, must be fixed then," and close the bug without further investigation.

Postponed

It's a fact of life that software is developed with limited resources. If you get more bugs than you can fix before the release date, some will have to be postponed. You might use this resolution for bugs that relate to features you're planning to implement in the future, or for bugs that you feel are unlikely to actually happen to real users (for example, crashing on a 10-million-character input in a text box is much more likely to happen in the test lab than in the real world).

If you find yourself using this resolution on serious bugs in core features that are part of what you're marketing for the current release, it's time to stop development and figure out how to adjust the feature set or the release date. Shipping code with known serious bugs is a good way to lose all of your customers.

If you know that you're targeting a bug fix or feature implementation for a particular release, there's an alternative to resolving the bug as postponed: you can just change the Fix For of the case to refer to the appropriate release. That way there's no chance that it will be forgotten. If you resolve the case as postponed, someone has to remember to reenter it into the system at the appropriate time.

Won't Fix

Won't Fix is the moral equivalent of postponing a bug forever. When you use this resolution, you're saying that you acknowledge the bug but that you don't consider it important enough to deserve any development effort. Perhaps you never expect it to happen in the real world, or perhaps you already know you're going to cut the feature that displays the bug. Be careful not to use this resolution too often to avoid demoralizing your application's testers.

Implemented

In response to a feature, this resolution is the same as using Fixed for a bug. If you mark a feature as implemented, you're saying that it now works as designed in the product. This is the resolution that you should see for most features.

Won't Implement

Some features will be entered into FogBugz by the project manager, working from an agreed-on design. Others, though, will come in from testers and random users. Not all of the latter type are really things that you should implement. Sooner or later, for example, someone will suggest adding the ability to read e-mail to almost any application. Unless this fits in with your vision of what the product should do, Won't Implement is an appropriate resolution.

Typically the Won't Implement decision should be made by a manager rather than a developer or tester. If you're a developer looking at a proposed feature and you think this is the right resolution, you may want to assign it to your manager with a comment urging that the feature not be implemented.

Already Exists

From time to time, you'll get suggestions for features that are already in the application. This resolution gives you an easy way to dispose of those suggestions. Maybe the feature was added after the build that's being tested, or maybe it's just hard for the tester to find. Before you use this resolution, though, think about whether there's something you ought to do to make the feature more discoverable. A feature that users can't find doesn't do anyone any good.

Responded

Some inquiries just require someone from customer service to write back, acknowledging the customer's concerns (or stating a policy such as "we don't comment on upcoming versions of the software, but you can apply for the beta program if you wish"). The Responded resolution exists as a way to close these cases.

Won't Respond

Sooner or later, most software houses attract attention from users who might charitably be called "cranks." If you get an inquiry demanding that you change your software to prevent the National Security Agency from using it to transmit mind-control messages via the keyboard, you should probably mark it Won't Respond and try to forget about it. That's assuming, of course, that your software doesn't actually transmit mind-control messages via the keyboard.

SPAM

This one is pretty self-explanatory. When you hand out an e-mail address, you'll get spam. This resolution is used to mark the spam.

■**Note** For more details on the way that FogBugz handles incoming e-mail and spam, refer to Chapter 5.

■**Caution** Depending on your mailbox settings, inquiries that are resolved as SPAM may be permanently, automatically, and irrevocably deleted after a certain number of days. This is necessary to keep your bug database from filling up with spam. But it does mean that you shouldn't use this resolution for cases that you actually want to keep track of.

Waiting For Info

Customers aren't always the best bug reporters in the world. You might get an inquiry that reads simply "it crashed." After sending back a request for more information, you'll probably want to resolve the inquiry as Waiting For Info so that it doesn't hang around in the system awaiting the customer, who may or may not actually write back.

Creating Release Notes

When you release that great new version of your software, your customers are going to want to know what's fixed and what new features you're giving them. FogBugz makes it easy to maintain release notes as you go along, effectively attaching a release note to any case. When you're done with a release, you can easily aggregate all of these notes into a single document.

■**Note** You will almost certainly not want to add release notes to every case. Some are too trivial for customers to care about. Others might reflect bugs that were introduced during development and fixed before any customer had a chance to see them, so customers will have no reason to care.

FogBugz does not attempt to compose release notes automatically based on the bug report, because bug reports are not usually worded the way you want your release notes to be worded. By the time you're done working on a case, the text of the bug might include internal code words, abbreviations, notes on competing products, and even rude back-and-forth between developers and testers. Rather than showing all of this junk to the end user, FogBugz requires you to create your own release notes specifically for this purpose.

You can add release notes to any case that has been resolved, whether it has been closed or not. When you open up a resolved case, you'll see a link at the top allowing you to edit release notes, as shown in Figure 4-13.

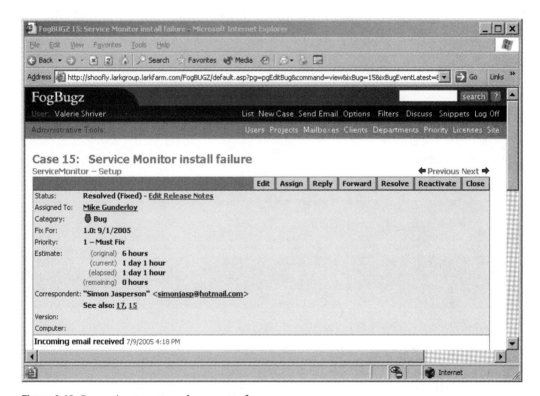

Figure 4-13. *Preparing to enter release notes for a case*

Click the link to open an editing screen, as shown in Figure 4-14.

To see all the release notes for a particular release, go to the FogBugz home screen by clicking the FogBugz icon in the top-left corner of any page, and then click the Release Notes link. Choose the release you are working on, and you will see a list of cases that were resolved for that release. From here you can jump to any case to edit its release notes. Figure 4-15 shows the release notes in progress for a particular release.

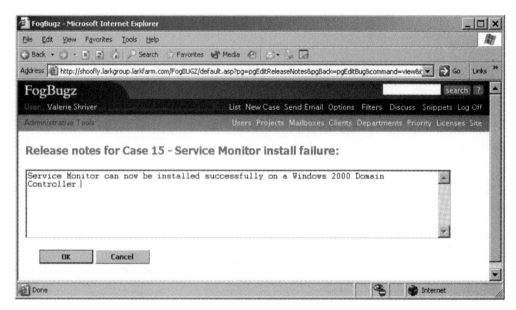

Figure 4-14. *Editing release notes for a case*

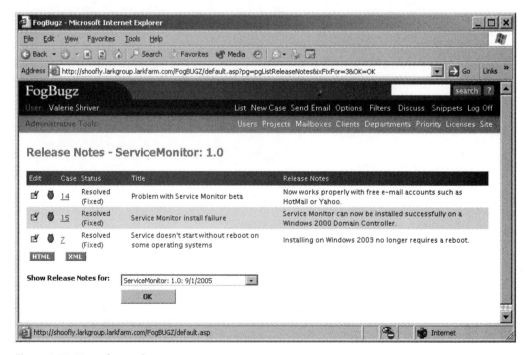

Figure 4-15. *Notes for a release*

At the bottom of this screen are two button links, one marked HTML and one marked XML. These icons are used to export the release notes to external files.

The HTML link displays all the release notes on one page. It uses extremely clean HTML with all formatting done in a style sheet. You can use your favorite HTML editor to format the release notes any way you like. By editing the styles, you can control the formatting of the entire release notes document to match your exact requirements. Figure 4-16 shows a set of release notes in HTML format.

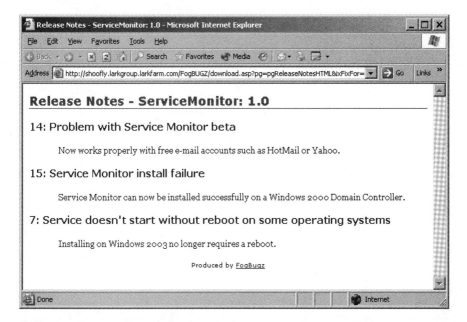

Figure 4-16. *HTML release notes*

The XML link displays the release notes in XML format, suitable for any further processing you may need to do to integrate the release notes with your Web site, documentation, or any other electronic interchange or content management system. Figure 4-17 shows a set of release notes in XML format.

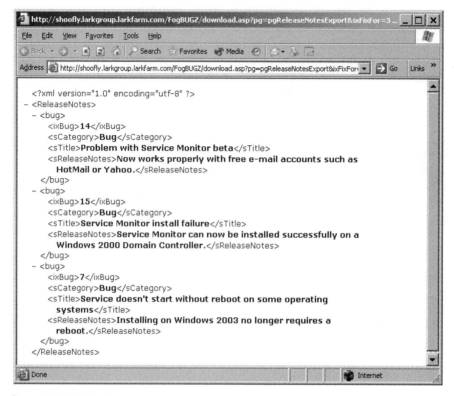

Figure 4-17. *XML release notes*

Extending FogBugz with Custom Reports

One of the great things about FogBugz is that all of the case information is kept in an open database—Access, SQL Server, or MySQL, depending on your installation. This means that you can use a variety of tools, including Microsoft Access, Microsoft Excel, Crystal Reports, and so on to drill into your FogBugz data. You'll need to have some facility with your tools to get sensible results out, and it helps to spend some time just exploring the FogBugz database so that you'll understand what's stored in the various tables. To conclude this chapter, I'll show you a couple of samples that might provoke further ideas.

Creating an Access Report

Suppose you'd like a nice-looking report listing all of the users in your database together with the count of cases assigned to each one, along with the status of those cases. Microsoft Access is ideal for preparing this sort of hierarchical report. To get started, open up your FogBugz database in Access.

■**Note** If you store FogBugz data in Access, you can open the database directly. If you're using SQL Server for your FogBugz database, you can create a new Access project based on the SQL Server data; search the Access help for "project" for more information. If you're using MySQL, you'll need to install the MySQL ODBC driver and attach the MySQL tables to an empty Access database to proceed.

Create a new Access query and add the Bug, Status, and Person table to the query. Figure 4-18 shows how these three tables can be joined (this particular screenshot is from an Access project based on a SQL Server FogBugz database).

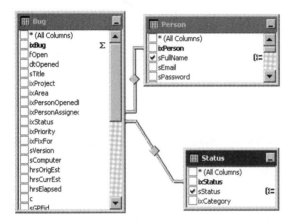

Figure 4-18. *Tables for building an Access query*

Select the ixBug field from the Bug table, the sStatus field from the Status table, and the sFullName field from the Person table. As you can see, FogBugz field and table names are very close to what you'll see on the user interface. Group the query on the sStatus and sFullName fields, and tell Access to count the ixBug field. The SQL for the query I'm using in this case is:

```
SELECT COUNT(Bug.ixBug) AS Count, Status.sStatus, Person.sFullName
FROM Bug INNER JOIN Status on Bug.ixStatus = Status.ixStatus
INNER JOIN Person on Bug.ixPersonAssignedTo = Person.ixPerson
GROUP BY Person.sFullName, Status.ixStatus
```

Save the query as BugCounts and close it. Navigate to the Queries container inside of Access, select the BugCounts query, and click the New Report button on the Access toolbar. Select the Report Wizard and click OK. On the first panel of the wizard, select all three fields for the report and click Next. On the second panel of the wizard, add sFullName and sStatus as grouping levels and click Next. On the third panel of the wizard, just click Next (you don't need to add any sorting because Access automatically sorts by the grouping fields). On the fourth panel of the wizard, select the Outline 2 layout and click Next. On the fifth panel of the wizard, select the Formal style and click Next. Click Finish to open the report. Figure 4-19 shows this report after a bit of editing in design view.

Case Count

Cases assigned to	Administrator		
Status	Active	2	**Bugs**

Cases assigned to	Ben Womack		
Status	Active	6	**Bugs**

Cases assigned to	CLOSED		
Status	Resolved (Duplicate)	1	**Bugs**
Status	Resolved (Fixed)	3	**Bugs**

Figure 4-19. *Access report based on FogBugz data*

Creating a Chart in Excel

Suppose you'd like some of the same information in a more graphical format. Excel provides a nice tool for graphs with a somewhat easier-to-use interface than Access. Here's how you can create a pie chart showing the number of cases currently assigned to each status.

First, fire up Excel. Then select Data ➤ Import External Data ➤ New Database Query. This will install Microsoft Query if necessary (it's not part of the default Excel installation) and then open the Choose Data Source dialog box. Select New Data Source and click OK. Name the data source and select the appropriate driver (Access or SQL Server), then connect to the database. Click OK to save the data source, then select it and click OK again. This will open the Query Wizard.

On the Choose Columns panel of the Query Wizard, expand the Bugs table and select the ixBug column. Then expand the Status table and select the sStatus column. Click Next twice, then click Finish to edit the query in Microsoft Query. Click the SQL toolbar button and modify the SQL statement:

```
SELECT Status.sStatus, Count(Bug.ixBug)
FROM Bug, Status
WHERE Bug.ixStatus = Status.ixStatus
GROUP BY Status.sStatus
```

Select Return Data to Microsoft Excel from the File menu. This will open the Import Data dialog box. You can now select where in the workbook to place the data; I chose to put it in the default A1 location.

After a moment, Excel will retrieve the data from FogBugz. Select the retrieved data and click the Chart Wizard button on the Excel toolbar. Select a chart type such as the 3D pie chart and click Finish to create the chart. Figure 4-20 shows a sample result.

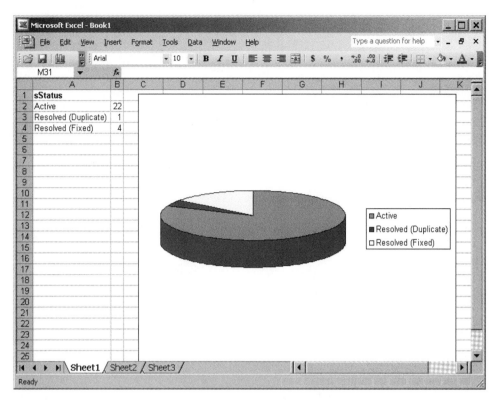

Figure 4-20. *Excel chart based on FogBugz data*

Summary

In this chapter, you learned about the FogBugz features that make it easier to manage and track an extensive caseload. You saw how estimates and due dates can be used to keep individual cases on track and how escalation reports can alert you to potential problems. E-mail and RSS notifications let you track bugs of interest without even opening FogBugz in your browser. I discussed the importance of carefully resolving bugs, and then showed you how to create release notes and custom reports.

But FogBugz isn't only a management tool; it's also a communications tool. In the next chapter, you'll learn how FogBugz integrates e-mail and discussion groups with its bug-tracking efforts, giving you a single way to manage customer interactions.

CHAPTER 5

■ ■ ■

Communicating with Customers

FogBugz is not just a piece of software for managing cases. It's also a support system for communicating with your customers. This communication happens in two ways. First, there's a comprehensive e-mail system that both allows e-mail into the system and sends responses back out. Second, there's a full-featured discussion group implementation. You can use discussion groups to gather customer feedback on new features, brainstorm new ways to market your product, or just provide a virtual place for people to relax and chat. In this chapter, I'll show you how to use these aspects of FogBugz.

Using E-Mail

You can use FogBugz for both internal e-mail (within your team) and external e-mail (with customers). I'll look at both of these aspects of the FogBugz e-mail system in turn.

Managing Internal E-Mail

FogBugz uses e-mail for team members in two ways. First, some bug notifications are automatically mailed to the appropriate team members. Second, you can decide that you're a glutton for punishment and sign up for even more e-mail if you want to.

Getting Automatic E-Mail from FogBugz

FogBugz will automatically send you e-mail about your cases. This means two things. First, if someone assigns a case to you, you'll get the e-mail shown in Figure 5-1.

Second, if someone edits a case that's already assigned to you, you'll get the e-mail shown in Figure 5-2.

FogBugz (Case 29) ServiceMonitor - Control Panel doesn't include company info after setup

fogbugz@example.com

To: Paige Nagel

A case was assigned to you in FogBugz.

Case ID: 29
Title: Control Panel doesn't include company info
after setup
Project: ServiceMonitor
Area: Setup
Priority: 2 - Must Fix
Release: 1.0: 9/1/2005
From: Valerie Shriver
URL:
http://shoofly.larkgroup.larkfarm.com/FogBUGZ/default.asp?
29
Last message:
There are properties in the MSI for this, aren't there?

If you do not want to receive automatic notifications from
FogBugz anymore, change your preferences in the Options
screen.
(http://shoofly.larkgroup.larkfarm.com/FogBUGZ/default.asp
?pg=pgPrefs)

Figure 5-1. *Notification of a new case assignment*

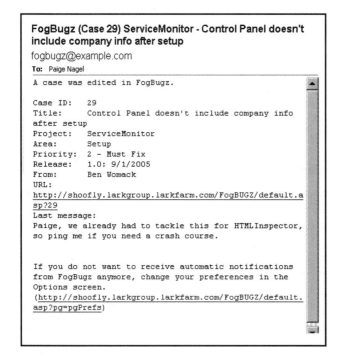

FogBugz (Case 29) ServiceMonitor - Control Panel doesn't include company info after setup

fogbugz@example.com

To: Paige Nagel

A case was edited in FogBugz.

Case ID: 29
Title: Control Panel doesn't include company info
after setup
Project: ServiceMonitor
Area: Setup
Priority: 2 - Must Fix
Release: 1.0: 9/1/2005
From: Ben Womack
URL:
http://shoofly.larkgroup.larkfarm.com/FogBUGZ/default.a
sp?29
Last message:
Paige, we already had to tackle this for HTMLInspector,
so ping me if you need a crash course.

If you do not want to receive automatic notifications
from FogBugz anymore, change your preferences in the
Options screen.
(http://shoofly.larkgroup.larkfarm.com/FogBUGZ/default.
asp?pg=pgPrefs)

Figure 5-2. *Notification of a change to a case*

In other words, FogBugz knows which cases you "own" and keeps you up to date on them (but it's smart enough not to e-mail you if you're the one making the change).

If you feel these e-mail notifications are too intrusive, you can turn them off for yourself by selecting Options on the main menu bar in FogBugz. Turn e-mail notifications off as shown in Figure 5-3 and click OK.

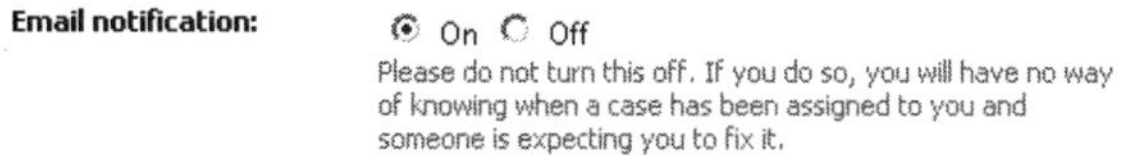

Email notification: ⊙ On ○ Off
Please do not turn this off. If you do so, you will have no way of knowing when a case has been assigned to you and someone is expecting you to fix it.

Figure 5-3. *Turning e-mail notifications off*

▪**Caution** It's not a great idea to turn off e-mail notifications. If you do so, you won't know when a new case has been assigned to you. I recommend you only turn notifications off if you already spend so much time in FogBugz that you won't miss changes anyhow, or if you're setting up a virtual account that doesn't correspond to a real human being. For example, you might want a FogBugz account where you can park cases that are intended for a new intern that you haven't hired yet. In that case, go ahead and turn off e-mail—but don't forget to turn it back on again!

Signing Up for Additional Notifications

On the other hand, perhaps you don't feel like you're getting enough mail. Never fear, if you're bored and lonely, FogBugz can help! At the very bottom of any case, you'll find a hyperlink to subscribe to the case, as shown in Figure 5-4.

Click the link and FogBugz will add you to the list of users to be notified by e-mail whenever anyone changes the case at all. You'll get e-mails similar to the one that you saw in Figure 5-2, just as if you were the owner of the case. When you visit a subscribed case in your browser, you'll see that the link changes to Unsubscribe to let you remove yourself from the notification list easily. Every e-mail also contains an unsubscription link.

In the interest of reducing the amount of unwanted e-mail, FogBugz does not let you force-subscribe someone else to a case. If you want them to know about it, you should temporarily assign the case to them with a note like "FYI" and then immediately assign it back to whomever it really belongs.

Before signing up for e-mail notifications, you should also consider the alternatives. First, because FogBugz changes the link to a case whenever anything changes about the case, you can monitor an entire list of cases simply by setting up an appropriate filter. Any cases that have changed in any way will be displayed with the unvisited link color (usually blue) in your browser.

The other alternative is to subscribe to a case using RSS. You can subscribe to all of the cases in a filter or to a single case by using RSS. For details on this technique, see the section "Using RSS Feeds" in Chapter 4.

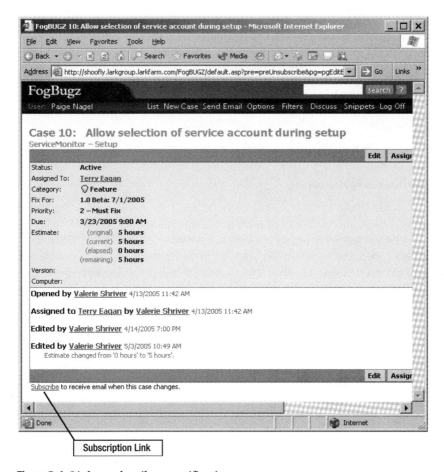

Figure 5-4. *Link to subscribe to notifications on a case*

Reminding People About Cases

I mentioned one other way to send e-mail to team members in Chapter 3, but it's worth bringing up here too. Sometimes, you may find that a whole list of cases is languishing in your FogBugz database. Perhaps some people are too busy to log in to FogBugz on a regular basis, or perhaps you have people with so many cases that they never get to the bottom of the list. While you're sorting out the management issues that lead to this situation, you can also remind people that you're waiting for them. Set up a filter that contains the cases of concern, then check them all on the case list page. Click the Remind button at the bottom of the screen to send e-mail to the users involved to remind them to look at their cases.

Managing Customer E-Mail

The internal e-mail features of FogBugz are simple to use: for the most part it just sends the e-mail you want when you want it. The customer-facing e-mail features are a good deal more complex. FogBugz incorporates extensive features for receiving, tracking, and responding to customer e-mail. You'll need to put in some effort to set up these features to work effectively for your own organization, but the payoff can be immense. In this section, I'll show you how to set up and use the customer-facing e-mail portion of FogBugz.

Overview of the Customer E-Mail Process

There's a lot to keep track of in understanding how e-mail integration works in FogBugz. If you get confused in the details, you might find it worthwhile to refer back to this summary. In outline, here's how it works:

- You set up a FogBugz mailbox and a corresponding POP3 mailbox.

- A message arrives in the mailbox on your mail server.

- Periodically, FogBugz uses the POP3 protocol to check your mail server for new messages.

- If it finds any messages, FogBugz downloads them from the mail server and creates a case out of each one.

- If you're using the AutoSort feature, FogBugz discards spam and sorts the rest of the messages into areas according to topic.

- If desired, FogBugz sends an immediate reply to the customer, providing them with a URL they can use to check on the status of their request.

- Once the message is in FogBugz, you can treat it like any other case: you can prioritize it, assign it, track it, and so on. You can also send a reply directly to the original e-mail sender from within the case.

- At any time, you can reply to the message from within FogBugz. FogBugz will insert the case number into the subject line of the outgoing message.

- If the customer responds to your reply, as long as they don't remove the FogBugz case number from the subject, their response will be appended to the current case rather than opening a new case.

- FogBugz will keep a complete transcript of everything that happens with the case, including all relevant incoming and outgoing e-mail and even private internal conversations about the case, which the customer does not see.

You can use FogBugz e-mail integration to manage customer service or a helpdesk. FogBugz can set automatic due dates on incoming e-mail so you can be certain that customers are receiving replies to their e-mail inquiries in a timely fashion.

Another use of FogBugz e-mail integration is to create a customer bug-reporting address or a suggestion box. Since all customer e-mails go right into FogBugz, you can treat them just like bugs or features: assign them to developers, schedule them, assign priorities and due dates, and so on. When the feature is implemented or the bug is fixed, with one click you can reply to the customer to notify them of this.

Setting up E-Mail Integration

To set up e-mail integration in FogBugz, you need to set up mailboxes. These are not POP3 mailboxes (though you require a POP3 mailbox that corresponds to each FogBugz mailbox), but FogBugz mailboxes. Each FogBugz mailbox corresponds to one incoming POP3 mailbox where FogBugz receives mail. You can set up as many mailboxes as you want; for example, you could set up customer-service@megautil.com as well as suggestions@megautil.com and bugs@megautil.com (at least, you could do that if you owned the megautil.com domain). Each mailbox can be treated differently.

Any FogBugz administrator can set up or edit mailboxes. To do so, log on as an administrator and select the Mailboxes link on the Administrative Tools bar. This will open the list of current mailboxes shown in Figure 5-5.

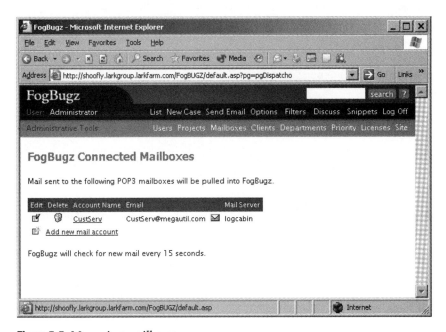

Figure 5-5. *Managing mailboxes*

From this screen, you can perform the following tasks:

- To edit an existing mailbox, click the edit icon or the mailbox name.

- To delete an existing mailbox, click the delete icon.

- To send test mail to a mailbox, click the envelope icon.

- To create a new mailbox, click the new icon or the Add new mail account hyperlink.

When you choose to create a new mailbox, you'll see the screen shown in Figure 5-6, which lets you configure the new mailbox. To configure a mailbox, you basically need to set up two things: where the e-mail comes from and what FogBugz should do with it. This involves setting up quite a number of options, but for many of them you should be able to use the defaults that FogBugz provides.

Figure 5-6. *Creating a new mailbox*

The first section of the page concerns account setup:

- Email address is the full e-mail address of the mailbox, for example, ServerMonitor@megautil.com. Messages that FogBugz sends will appear to come from this account.

- Full name is the full name that will appear when replying to e-mail from this mailbox, for example, MegaUtil Customer Service. Automated mail will always come from this name. If you send mail manually (by hitting the Reply button while you're working with a case), FogBugz will offer you a choice between this name and your own name. This allows you to choose between hiding behind an anonymous alias and providing the customer with personalized feedback.

- Account Name is the login account on the POP3 mail server. FogBugz won't set this account up for you. There are just too many different e-mail servers. But your network administrator should be able to set up as many POP3 accounts as you need.

- Password is the login password on the POP3 mail server.

- Mail Server is the DNS name or IP address of the POP3 mail server.

- Port is the TCP port for the POP3 service. This is almost always 110 unless you're using secure POP3, which is almost always 995.

The next section of the mailbox configuration screen handles automatic replies. Figure 5-7 shows this portion of the screen.

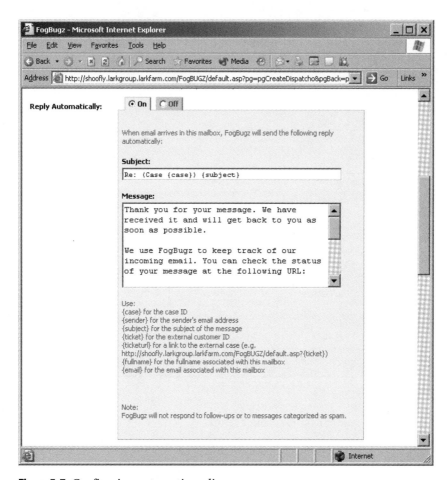

Figure 5-7. *Configuring automatic replies*

You can click the Off radio button to simply disable automatic replies, in which case all of the other options vanish. But if you leave automatic replies on, you can set up these options:

- Subject is the subject line to be used for automatic replies.

- Message is the message to be sent as an automatic reply.

It might seem like this is a mighty inflexible way to set up automatic replies, but there's a trick: FogBugz accepts a number of shortcuts that will automatically be expanded when the e-mail is sent. You can use any of these shortcuts to make your automatic replies more flexible:

- {case} for the Case ID.

- {email} for the e-mail return address of the FogBugz mailbox.

- {fullname} for the full name associated with the FogBugz mailbox.

- {sender} for the sender's e-mail address (that is, the person who sent the e-mail that triggered the automatic reply).

- {subject} for the subject of the original message.

- {ticket} for the external ticket ID. This is a randomized identifier that's hard to guess.

- {ticketurl} for a full external link to the case.

- {url} for the base URL of the FogBugz server.

The default message supplied by FogBugz is straightforward:

```
Thank you for your message. We have received it and will
get back to you as soon as possible.

We use FogBugz to keep track of our incoming email.
You can check the status of your message at the following URL:

    {ticketurl}

Please reply to this message if there's anything else
we can do for you.

--
{fullname}
{email}
----------------------------------------------------------
Powered by FogBugz from Fog Creek Software.
http://www.fogcreek.com/FogBugz
```

While you can use this message as-is, you probably want to customize it to include at least your company name. You might also want to eliminate the FogBugz ad, though having it there does help tip people off that this is an automatic reply.

■**Tip** No matter what you do, please make sure the outgoing subject includes (Case {case}) because this will ensure that if the customer replies to the autoreply, their reply will go into the same case number instead of opening a new case.

■**Note** FogBugz will not respond to follow-ups or to messages it decides are spam. It will also not respond to certain bulk e-mail like "out of office" notices, and it won't send more than three autoreplies an hour to the same person, to prevent autoreply loops.

The remaining options let you fine-tune the way that FogBugz handles messages:

- Due lets you set a due date in the case that's created when the message comes in. You can leave this set to None (the default), in which case FogBugz won't automatically assign a due date. Alternatively, you can choose Automatic, and then select a particular number of hours, working hours, days, or working days to be used when calculating the automatic due date.

- Sort Messages lets you determine how incoming messages are categorized. If you leave this set to the default FogBugz Autosort, then FogBugz will use its own sorting engine to categorize incoming messages. See the section "Sorting Messages" later in this chapter for more details. Alternatively, you can select Manual sorting, in which case you'll be prompted to supply values for Project, Area, Fix For, Priority, User to Open the Case As, and Initial Assignment. These values will then be used for every message that arrives in the mailbox.

- Message Template allows you to set up a signature that will be automatically inserted at the bottom of every reply you send in this mailbox. This textbox accepts the same set of shortcut values as the message textbox that I discussed earlier.

- Delete spam after lets you avoid spam filling up your FogBugz database. Any message that is either resolved as SPAM or moved into the Spam area will be deleted after the number of days that you set here, which defaults to 7 days. If you don't want to delete spam, leave this blank.

- Delete inquiries after lets you set up FogBugz to delete the complete case history of all closed inquiries after a certain number of days if you do not wish to keep a permanent record of incoming e-mail.

When you've filled in all of the configuration options, click OK to create the new mailbox. FogBugz will start checking it for mail immediately. As FogBugz receives e-mail messages, it discards the ones that it decides are spam (though you can reverse that decision if you need to) and then creates cases from the rest. Once an e-mail turns into a case, you can work with it just like you can with any other case in the system.

■**Tip** When you are looking at an e-mail from a customer, at the top of the case, you'll see a list of all the other e-mails you've ever received from the exact same e-mail address in the Correspondent section. You can also search for other e-mail from the same domain name by clicking the link to the right of the @ sign in the e-mail address. This is helpful because sometimes multiple people will correspond with you from the same company, and this trick will find all their messages.

Using Snippets

Once you've got e-mail coming into your system, you're going to want to reply to it. Some of the incoming e-mails will be complete bug reports, but other e-mails will be confusing complaints, suggestions for future features, or just plain irrelevancies. If you try to reply to all of this mail, you'll soon find yourself saying the same things over and over. Fortunately, FogBugz offers a shortcut here.

FogBugz lets you set up *snippets*. A snippet can be anything from a word or two ("Sincerely yours") to a complete form letter. When you are replying to an e-mail, you simply type the name of the snippet followed by a backtick (`), and the snippet will be inserted for you automatically.

Snippets can be used to make it very easy to reply to frequently asked questions with a canned reply or form letter. This has two benefits. First, it cuts down on the amount of typing that you (or anyone else) has to do to put together a response. Second, it lets you use and reuse a response that has been carefully edited and checked over by those concerned. This cuts down on typographical errors, support people not sticking to the marketing message, and developers accidentally leaking the next big feature before it's announced.

There are two kinds of snippets: snippets for everybody, which are set up by an administrator for the whole team to use, and personal snippets, which only work for a single FogBugz user. If you log on as an administrator and then click the Snippets link in the main toolbar, you'll see the screen shown in Figure 5-8.

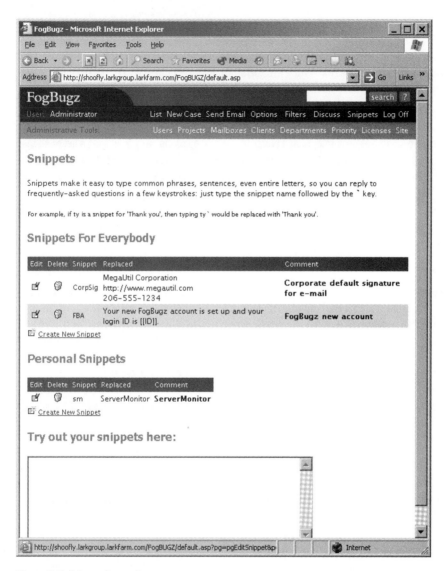

Figure 5-8. *Managing snippets*

Administrators will see two lists of snippets here; regular users will only see their own personal snippets. In either list, you can perform these actions:

- To edit a snippet, click the edit icon.

- To delete a snippet, click the delete icon.

- To create a new snippet, click the new icon or the Create New Snippet hyperlink.

The snippet management page also has a handy textbox where you can try out snippets. Type the name of a snippet followed by the snippet activation key to test out the snippet in this space. Or press the snippet key twice (``) to browse a list of snippets, as shown in Figure 5-9.

This feature works anywhere that snippets do, and is especially handy if you can't remember which snippet you want.

Figure 5-9. *Browsing snippets*

The Create New Snippet hyperlink will take you to the screen shown in Figure 5-10. To create a new snippet, assign the snippet a name and replacement text, as well as a comment to be shown on the snippet list page. Then click OK to create the snippet.

■**Tip** FogBugz won't let you create two snippets with the same name. There is one exception to this rule: you may create a personal snippet with the same name as a global snippet. In that case, the personal snippet will be used instead of the corresponding global snippet, until you delete the personal snippet or change the name of one of the two snippets.

Each user can change the key that is used to activate snippets in the Options screen. By default FogBugz uses `` ` ``, which is conveniently located in the top-left corner of an American computer keyboard. The other symbols you can choose are

\

<

>

#

~

*

^

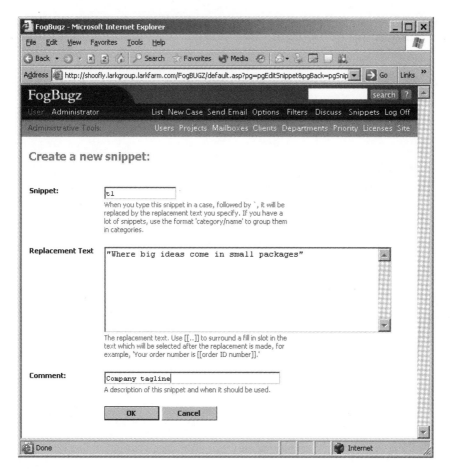

Figure 5-10. *Creating a new snippet*

If a snippet contains a section surrounded by [[and]], that section will be highlighted after you insert the snippet on most Web browsers. This is extremely useful when you want to insert something in the middle of a snippet. For example, if snippet b is defined as

```
I have looked up your account number and your
current balance is $[[x]]. Thank you for contacting us.
```

you can type **b`24** to produce

```
I have looked up your account number and your
current balance is $24. Thank you for contacting us.
```

Sorting Messages

Ever faced an inbox full of messages and needed to sort them out between various folders to keep track of them? Ever wished you had an assistant to help you out with the job? Well, in

FogBugz, you do. FogBugz contains a sophisticated spam-blocking algorithm that learns how to recognize spam automatically as you train it. Beyond that, though, FogBugz can also sort your incoming e-mail into categories other than Spam and Not Spam. Setting up and training FogBugz AutoSort can be a bit time-consuming, but it's well worth the effort.

FogBugz uses an adaptive system for recognizing spam and otherwise sorting the incoming e-mail. This means that rather than using a fixed set of spam clues (such as assuming that "mortgage" must mean spam), it learns from your own incoming e-mail. If you work for a bank, "mortgage" probably doesn't mean spam.

In addition to using positive clues (for example, "V1agra" probably means spam), FogBugz will learn from negative clues as well (for example, if the e-mail contains the name of one of your products, it's much less likely to be spam). FogBugz examines many aspects of the incoming e-mail for clues that could be considered positive signs of spam, negative signs of spam, or neutral. And because you train it, FogBugz will also adapt itself to the particular stream of e-mail that you receive.

▓Note FogBugz implements a modified version of the Bayesian filtering algorithm proposed by Paul Graham in the articles "A Plan for Spam" and "Better Bayesian Filtering" (both available at http://www.paulgraham.com), with modifications and improvements designed by Ben Kamens, a summer intern at Fog Creek.

When you first configure a mailbox and turn on FogBugz AutoSort, FogBugz sets up a project named Inbox with three areas: Spam, Not Spam, and Undecided. At first, FogBugz AutoSort has no clues at all about what messages are spam and what messages are not spam. All incoming messages are put straight into the Undecided area. FogBugz automatically sets up an Inbox filter, so to get to the Inbox you can just click the link on your FogBugz home page. Figure 5-11 shows what the Inbox might look like after a few messages arrive.

FogBugz creates the Inbox project with three predefined areas: NotSpam (for messages that it is sure aren't spam), Spam (for messages that it is sure are spam), and Undecided (for everything else). One of the neat things about FogBugz AutoSort is that it's not limited to these three categories. You can create up to 14 custom areas to go along with these three. For example, if you use the same e-mail alias for job applications and tech support, you might create areas called Job Applications and Tech Support.

▓Tip The fewer custom areas you create, the more reliable the AutoSort function will be.

If you are trying to sort messages into different areas, you will have the best luck if there are obvious clues in the message. For example, if you make an area for accounting, various words like "Invoice" and "Receipt" and "Payment" may be good clues that an incoming e-mail goes to the accounting area, and AutoSort will pick up on these clues automatically as you train it.

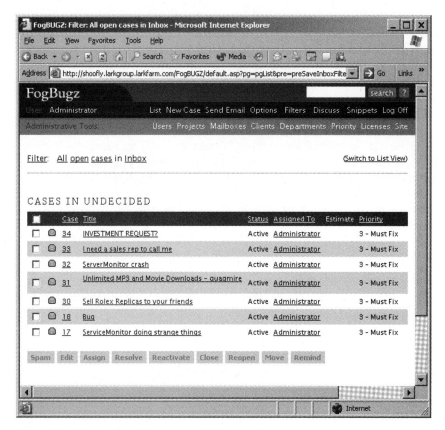

Figure 5-11. *Messages waiting in the FogBugz Inbox*

■**Tip** When you first set up AutoSort on a mailbox in FogBugz, FogBugz will create a project named Inbox and add the areas Spam, Not Spam, and Undecided to the project. But you're not limited to this default inbox. You can turn any project into an inbox by telling AutoSort to start placing mail in that project. As soon as you do, the Spam, Not Spam, and Undecided areas will show up in that project too.

However, all artificial intelligence algorithms have their limitations, and there may be cases where AutoSort simply can't figure out a good enough clue from the message as to which area it should go in. For example, if you try to train AutoSort to separate messages based on Republican customers versus Democratic customers, it might never be able to do this because there are no consistent clues in the message to do this sorting.

To make AutoSort useful, you need to train it. To train AutoSort, you need to teach it about every message in the Undecided area, either by flagging it as spam or moving it to the appropriate area if it's not spam. There are two ways to move a case to the Spam folder. First, you can select as many cases as you like in the list view of the Inbox and click the Spam button beneath the list. This will mark all of the selected cases as spam and get them out of your sight forever.

But if you're not sure, go ahead and open the case by clicking its title. This will open it in the regular FogBugz editing screen, as shown in Figure 5-12.

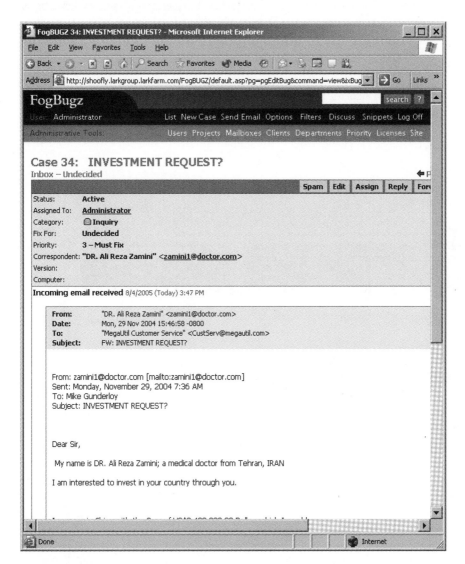

Figure 5-12. *Spam or ham?*

If the message is spam, click the Spam button to get rid of it. This will return you to the list of messages in the Inbox. On the other hand, if the message is something you actually need to deal with, you can move it to the correct area by editing the case, just as you would with any other case, or use the Move button at the bottom of the Inbox.

Tip For safety, FogBugz never displays HTML mail as HTML—it always shows you the plain text version. Merely viewing an e-mail can never run scripts or otherwise compromise your system's security. However, as with all e-mail, use extreme caution when opening or saving any attachment unless you know who it is from and you were expecting it.

After you've classified all of the messages in the Inbox, your screen will look something like Figure 5-13. Note that the spam messages aren't shown here. After a few days, the system will delete them entirely so that they don't clutter your database. Also, if you've moved any cases to another project, they'll no longer be listed in the Inbox.

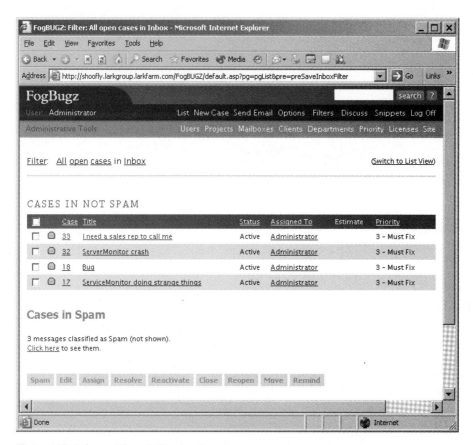

Figure 5-13. *Inbox with sorted messages*

After a few days, you should notice that AutoSort is correctly sorting most messages. In the first few days, there is a small chance that a few messages will be mistakenly flagged as spam. Don't worry about this, but do move them into the Not Spam area to help train FogBugz AutoSort. In fact, any time you see a message in the wrong area, take the time to move it to the right area. The more accurately you classify messages, the more easily AutoSort will take over the job from you.

After you've received a bunch of spam and a bunch of good messages, typically after a couple of days or about 100–200 messages, you'll find that AutoSort is doing a really good job automatically sorting messages. But no matter how good it gets, it will always be undecided about some messages and you'll have to decide those cases yourself. That's because AutoSort tries to be conservative to avoid accidentally flagging a message as spam when it's not really spam.

■**Caution** It is extremely rare for FogBugz AutoSort to accidentally mark something as spam that is a legitimate e-mail. In fact, our experience is that it's more common for humans to mistake a real e-mail for spam than for FogBugz AutoSort to make this mistake! Unfortunately, there's always the possibility that a legitimate e-mail from a customer will look so "spammy" that it gets deleted accidentally. If you are concerned about this, set aside some time to review the spam messages every few days just to be certain nothing legitimate is getting lost.

Replying to E-Mail and Sending E-Mail

FogBugz also lets you communicate directly with customers via e-mail. By keeping customer communications in FogBugz, rather than in your own mailbox on an Exchange or other e-mail server, you can make them available to the entire team. Think of this as creating a repository of knowledge that everyone can draw on. It's much easier to discover if a problem has already been solved for another customer, for example, if all e-mail about customer problems is kept in one place.

It's easy to contact a customer who has submitted a case to FogBugz via e-mail. If you open such a case in FogBugz, the action buttons at the top of the case include Reply and Forward. If you click the Reply button, FogBugz will open a special editor in the case, as shown in Figure 5-14.

You can choose whether the reply should come from the default name for the mailbox or from your own name, and you can edit the message header and message as you like. Remember, you should leave the case number as a part of the subject so that FogBugz can automatically attach any customer reply to the same case. You can also attach a file to your reply if you like. Click the Send & Close or Send button to send the mail. In either case, your message will be saved as part of the notes on the case.

Clicking Forward opens the same form, except that it does not automatically grab the e-mail address of the original submitter as the destination for the e-mail. This lets you use e-mail to get a copy of the bug to anyone on e-mail (perhaps an executive for whom you haven't bothered to buy a FogBugz license, for example).

Regular cases (those that did not come into the system through a FogBugz mailbox) don't have the Reply and Forward buttons. Instead, they have an Email button, which opens up an e-mail form in the notes for the case, similar to the one you'd get from forwarding a mailed case.

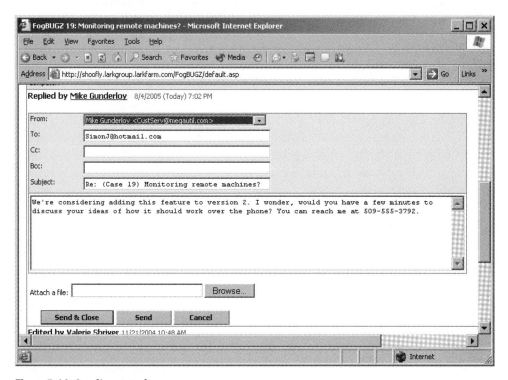

Figure 5-14. *Sending a reply to a customer*

You can also send e-mail to a customer without having a FogBugz case already open. To initiate e-mail to a customer, click Send Email in the main toolbar. This does two things. First, it creates a new case, just as if you'd clicked the New Case link. Second, it opens an e-mail form as the first note on the new case, as if you'd decided to e-mail it after you opened it. So the Send Email link doesn't do anything that you couldn't do otherwise, but it lets you skip a few manual steps. As with any other e-mail exchange, any replies from that customer will automatically be appended to the end of the new case so that everyone else on your team can see the entire history of the e-mail transaction.

When you've got a team of people replying to customer e-mail, there's always a risk that two people will try to respond to the same message at the same time. At best, this can make you look unprofessional; at worst, it can severely confuse your customers. FogBugz prevents this in two ways:

- As soon as you hit the Reply button, the case is assigned to you. That way other people can see that you're working on it.

- If somebody else dashes in and sends a reply anyway while you are in the process of composing your reply, FogBugz won't actually send your reply when you click Send. Instead, it will warn you that somebody else has changed the case and let you decide if you still want to send your reply or cancel it.

Using Discussion Groups

E-mail provides an excellent way to communicate one-on-one with your customers in private. Although you can include multiple recipients for a single e-mail or cut and paste e-mail to a Web site, the fact remains that e-mail is ill-suited for discussions involving many people or for those that you want to be easily accessible. Enter discussion groups. With version 4.0, FogBugz introduces a full-fledged discussion group feature.

FogBugz lets you set up both private (available only to logged-in users) and public (available to anyone who can see the server via the Internet) discussion groups. Private discussion groups are a great way to communicate in your team. Unlike private e-mail, once conversations are captured in a discussion group, they will always be visible and searchable, capturing valuable development knowledge for posterity.

Public discussion groups are a great way to announce features, collect ideas, and provide tech support for customers. There are some big advantages to using discussion groups for these purposes instead of e-mail:

- If the same problem comes up frequently, you won't have to repeat yourself.

- Customers won't hesitate to tell you if you plan to do something stupid, providing valuable feedback as you plan for the future.

- There's a good chance that another customer will help a customer with a problem before you have a chance to get to them.

In addition to keeping a visible history of a conversation, FogBugz also lets you link items in discussion groups to cases so that you can make sure somebody deals with each customer problem, bug report, and feature request. Figure 5-15 shows a discussion group in action. This is the view that a user logged in to FogBugz gets. As you can see, anyone can contribute to this public discussion group. FogBugz users can turn posts into cases and take other actions that I'll discuss later in this chapter.

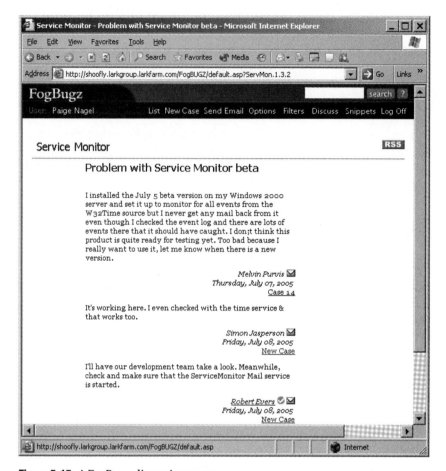

Figure 5-15. *A FogBugz discussion group*

Setting Up Discussion Groups

Any FogBugz administrator can set up discussion groups, and there's no practical technical limit to the number of discussion groups that you can create. The real limit is social: how many discussion groups can you effectively manage? If there are too many discussion groups, it will be harder to get a critical mass of people in any one of them. My recommendation is to start with only one or two groups; you can always create more later if you find a good reason to do so.

To set up a new discussion group, click the Discuss link on the main toolbar and then select the Customize option from the drop-down list. This will open the screen shown in Figure 5-16.

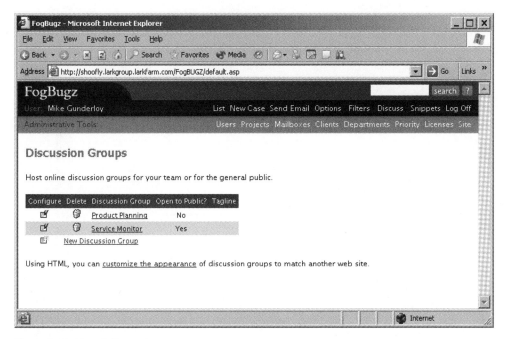

Figure 5-16. *List of discussion groups*

This screen shows all of the discussion groups that FogBugz is currently managing. From here, you can perform several functions:

- To configure a discussion group, click the configure icon or the discussion group name.

- To delete a discussion group, click the delete icon.

- To create a new discussion group, click the new icon or the New Discussion Group link.

- To customize the appearance of discussion groups, click the customize the appearance link (see the section "Customizing Discussion Group Appearance" later in this chapter for more details).

Creating a new discussion group opens the screen shown in Figure 5-17.

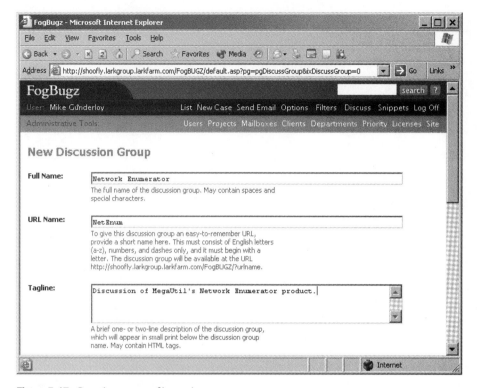

Figure 5-17. *Creating a new discussion group*

To set up a new discussion group, you'll need to configure the following options:

- Full Name is a complete name for the discussion group that will appear as a headline. You can use spaces and special characters in the full name.

- URL Name is a short name for the discussion group that is incorporated into a simplified URL people can use to access the discussion group. For example, if your URL name is plans and your web server is running at http://fogbugz.megautil.com, this discussion group will be located at http://fogbugz.megautil.com/?plans (notice the question mark).

- Tagline lets you supply a brief description of the discussion group (or any other small bit of text), which will appear below the discussion group name. The tagline may contain HTML tags.

- Sidebar lets you supply text that will appear in the left-hand sidebar of the discussion group. The sidebar may contain HTML tags. This can be used to make links to other popular locations, to provide guidelines and FAQs, or for a decorative picture.

- Posting Guidelines lets you supply text that will appear right below the message text entry field on new messages, telling people some basic rules for posting to the discussion group. The default text of "Don't use HTML. Surround URLs with spaces" is a good starting point. The posting guidelines may contain HTML tags. If your rules get too long, don't expect people to read them!

- Days on Home Page is a number determining how many days' worth of topics will be listed on the main page. For busy discussion groups, use a low number like 7 to keep the main page manageable. For new discussion groups, 30 is a good start. Anything older than this number of days will disappear from the main page (although it will still be visible in the archive). While your discussion group builds up critical mass, you should adjust this number up to make the group look busier and avoid the dreaded "empty restaurant syndrome" in which nobody bothers posting to the group because it looks deserted.

- Sort Posts determines whether to let AutoSort look at every incoming post, delete the spam, and hold suspicious posts for a moderator to approve. I recommend you leave this setting on.

- Open to Public determines whether you need to be logged on to FogBugz to participate in the discussion group. Otherwise, anyone who can navigate to your FogBugz server can participate.

Customizing Discussion Group Appearance

FogBugz allows you to customize virtually every aspect of the visual appearance of the discussion groups so as to match your corporate Web site exactly. However, this customization requires some skill with HTML and CSS. To get started, click the Customize the Appearance link on the screen that lists all of the discussion groups. This will take you to a new screen where you can enter these options:

- *Top of the Page*: HTML that will be inserted before the discussion group content.

- *Bottom of the Page*: HTML that will be inserted after the discussion group content. This is where the default FogBugz advertisement is located, which you can remove if you like.

- *Customize Styles*: CSS to be added to discussion pages, which lets you change the style of any page element.

- *Left Sidebar Width*: The width (in pixels) of the left sidebar. This defaults to 125.

- *Main Body Width*: The width (in pixels) of the body of the discussion group. The default value is 600.

■**Note** Any customization settings made here apply to all discussion groups on the server.

Starting a New Topic

After you've set up a discussion group, anyone navigating to the group's home page will see a screen like the one shown in Figure 5-18.

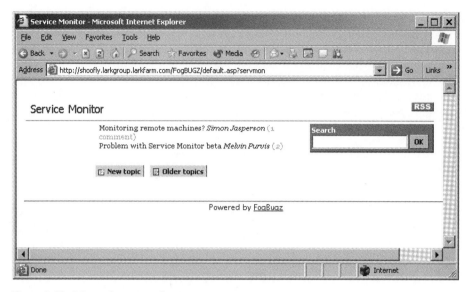

Figure 5-18. *Discussion group home page*

▓**Note** Figure 5-18 shows a public discussion group as seen by a non-FogBugz user. If you're logged in to FogBugz when you visit a discussion group, you'll see the same content, but it will be wrapped with the normal FogBugz menus.

You can perform a number of actions from this home page:

- See the content in an existing topic by clicking the topic name.

- Create a new topic by clicking the New Topic link.

- See topics that have scrolled off the home page by clicking the Older Topics link.

- Search for content anywhere in the discussion group by entering text in the search box and clicking OK.

- Subscribe to an RSS feed for the entire discussion group from the RSS icon.

When you click the link to create a new topic, FogBugz will display the screen shown in Figure 5-19.

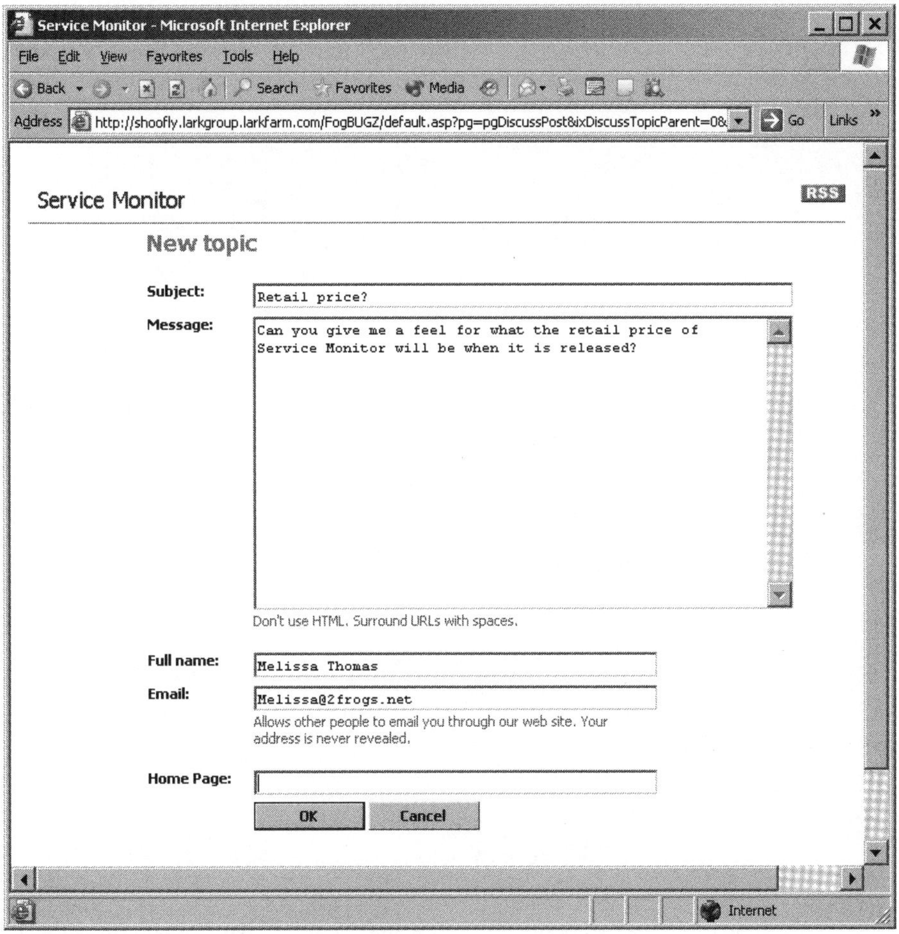

Figure 5-19. *Creating a new discussion topic*

To create a new discussion topic, you need to supply a subject and a message that will be used to kick off the discussion. You also need to fill in your own name and (optionally) an e-mail address and Web site where you can be contacted.

Tip FogBugz never reveals users' e-mail addresses on the Web site, so they can't be harvested by spam-bots. Instead, it turns addresses into a hyperlink that other users can click to enter messages. FogBugz then forwards those messages to the user, and it's up to the recipient to decide whether to respond. FogBugz will not forward more than five personal e-mails from each sender per day, to make spam scripts impossible.

The new topic will be created as soon as you click OK, and you'll be able to see the message that you entered immediately. Figure 5-20 shows the start of a new discussion topic. The little envelope is the hyperlink to send e-mail to this user.

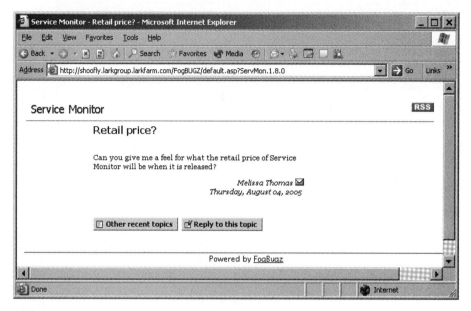

Figure 5-20. *A new topic, ready for discussion*

Replying to a Topic

To reply to a topic in a discussion group, click the topic's link on the discussion group home page. This will open a page that shows all of the current discussion on the topic, with the newest entries at the bottom of the page. At the very end of the page, you'll find a Reply to this topic button. This opens the screen shown in Figure 5-21. Note that you're not shown the previous discussion at the time that you're entering your reply. I'll talk about the reasons for this later in the chapter.

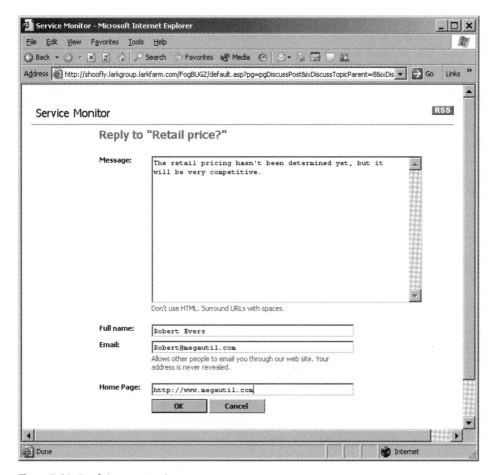

Figure 5-21. *Replying to a topic*

Managing Discussion Groups

Hopefully your own team members will be polite and stay on topic in the private discussion groups on your server. But as soon as you open a discussion group to the public, you're likely to see two things:

- *Spam*: Spammers are getting good at posting advertisements and other spam to public discussion groups as soon as they find them, even rarely used discussion groups on quiet corners of the Internet with no visitors. They often try to post URLs to their own Web site in hopes of improving the Google PageRank of those URLs.

- *General abuse*: This ranges from personal abuse to copyright violations to merely off-topic posts.

Fortunately, FogBugz lets you use AutoSort to help keep this sort of nonsense under control. If you leave AutoSort turned on for a discussion group, it will take a look at all messages before they get posted, and if necessary quarantine them for approval, or even delete them. Anyone who is logged on to FogBugz as an administrator will be able to moderate discussion groups, removing abusive posts and spam. Over time, as you moderate groups manually, AutoSort will learn from your moderation and try to mimic what you did. For example, if it sees that you keep deleting posts from a certain IP address or posts containing a certain word, it will learn to delete those automatically. That way the post is deleted before it even appears.

FogBugz AutoSort is not 100% reliable, and sometimes it will be suspicious about a post but not certain that it needs to be deleted. In this case, it will merely hold the post for approval. A post that is held for approval will not appear to the outside world until a moderator clears it. Alternatively, the moderator can decide the post should be deleted as spam, and AutoSort will learn more about what you consider to be spam.

If you're an administrator, going to a discussion group home page from within FogBugz will show you a view like the one in Figure 5-22. In addition to the information that any user can see, the administrator is also told about posts that have been held or deleted by AutoSort (one of each appears in this figure).

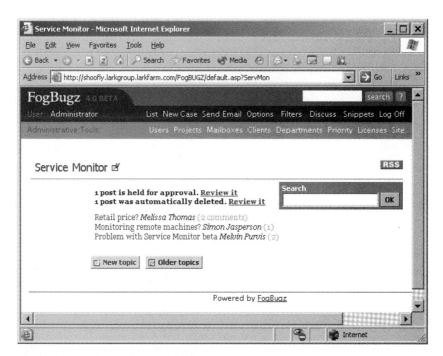

Figure 5-22. *Moderator's view of a discussion group*

Each of the categories of posts has its own review link. When you click the review link, you'll see a screen such as the one in Figure 5-23. Posts that are held for approval are marked, and posts that were deleted automatically are shown in strikeout type and also marked.

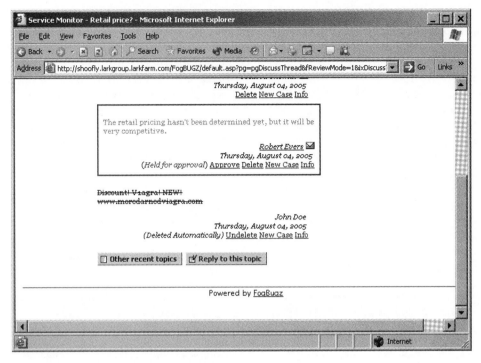

Figure 5-23. *Moderating a discussion group*

Moderators are all-powerful. For a regular discussion group item, they can

- Delete the item.

- Create a new case from the item.

- Click the info link to see the e-mail address and IP address of the poster.

For an item that has been held for approval, they can

- Approve the item, making it visible to everyone.

- Delete the item.

- Create a new case from the item.

- Click the info link to see the e-mail address and IP address of the poster.

For an item that has been deleted, they can

- Undelete the item.

- Create a new case from the item.

- Click the info link to see the e-mail address and IP address of the poster.

Creating cases from items is one of the most powerful parts of the integration of discussion groups with FogBugz. As you saw in Chapter 1, this gives you an easy way to capture a bug report from a customer—even when that customer isn't part of a formal beta program. You can turn any feedback into a case to track it for later. You can also allow your team to use this feature to assign discussion group items among themselves to make sure that every topic gets a reply. When you create a case from an item, FogBugz also creates hyperlinks in both directions to make it easy to go from one to the other.

As the moderator deletes posts, undeletes posts, and approves posts that were held for approval, FogBugz AutoSort will learn from those actions. Over time, it will become more adept at recognizing the signs of bad posts, as well as the signs of good posts. So after a while, you won't have as much need to actively moderate a discussion group.

Whenever a post has been deleted, the original person who made that post will still see it if they log on from the same IP address or the same web browser. This technique helps reduce the number of people who become furious at having their precious post deleted and try to disrupt the discussion group in other ways.

FogBugz also uses a number of tactics to try to prevent spam from overwhelming a discussion group:

- It does not allow Google or other well-behaved search engine spiders to follow links in the discussion group to outside URLs, so posting an outside URL will not increase the Google PageRank of that URL.

- It does not allow new replies to topics that have already scrolled off the home page, so spammers cannot hide spam in old messages, which the moderator is unlikely to see.

- It uses AutoSort to spot and block spam.

- It prevents users from finding out that their message was blocked or deleted. If spammers notice their spam is being blocked, they will try to work around the block and try to repost their spam using different words. However since FogBugz continues to show even deleted messages to the IP address range of the person (if spammers are people) who posted it, it's very hard for spammers to even find out that their spam is being removed.

Moderating Effectively

As your discussion community grows, it becomes increasingly likely that you will find a small number of disruptive users (or that they will find you; some people seem to wander from system to system looking for places to cause trouble). Whether out of malice, boredom, or greed, somebody will try to abuse your discussion system. As soon as you delete their posts, they will immediately appear under another name complaining about censorship and prattling about their First Amendment right to advertise sex aids and talk about politics on your software discussion board. Inevitably, this will bring in a chorus of naive but well-meaning users quoting Voltaire who didn't see the porn ad that got deleted, but they sure know they are against censorship.

You may find this whole thing to be fun, or you may just find it a boring distraction from real work. If left unchecked, like Usenet, any public discussion group will rapidly accumulate a significant amount of spam and "noise." The noise itself will drive away the best users, and the signal-to-noise ratio will worsen.

To address these issues, it's best to apply some simple rules:

- Moderate your discussion group regularly. An unmoderated discussion group tends to drift off topic in ever wider swings.

- Don't delete things merely because you disagree with them; reserve the Delete button for things that are really off topic or abusive. Although FogBugz tries to prevent people from finding out that their posts were deleted so they won't launch into a full-scale attack, a small percentage of your users will have access to the discussion group from different IP addresses, so they will discover that their posts are being deleted.

- On the other hand, don't be afraid to delete things just because they are off topic. If you're running a technical support discussion group, go ahead and get rid of the political ads and the ruminations about which fast food joint is best and the pointers to the latest Evil Doings of Big Government. There are plenty of other places where people can go to discuss those things. (If you find your users complaining vociferously, you might try setting up an explicitly off-topic discussion group to satisfy them.)

- Help train FogBugz AutoSort whenever possible. It's always better if a post is deleted instantly by FogBugz AutoSort before anyone sees it, because it reduces the number of people who even notice that moderation is taking place and launch into predictable rants about censorship.

- Train FogBugz AutoSort to delete any posts that are about deleted posts, censorship, and forum mechanics. They are off topic and sure to stir people up. If you don't do this, you'll keep repeating the conversation about censorship every three weeks as new users join in, which will eventually bore the old users, driving the good users away from the discussion group and attracting the bad ones.

Understanding FogBugz Discussion Groups

There are many, many software packages out there that support discussion groups. So why does FogBugz have its own? There are two good reasons for this. First, coupling discussion groups to the case-tracking system gives you a really easy way to find customer complaints and ideas and move them into the system where you can act on them. Second, the folks at Fog Creek had some particular ideas about how a discussion group should be run, and they wanted a product to implement those ideas.

The result is that FogBugz discussion groups act like other discussion packages in some ways, but are unique in others. Although you can always hack around in the FogBugz source code to change the way that discussion groups behave, it's worth understanding some of the design decisions here before you do so. You might find, on reflection, that you like things just the way they are. As you read through the rest of this chapter, keep in mind the primary axiom of online communities:

Small software implementation details result in big differences in the way the community develops, behaves, and feels.

One thing you'll notice is that the discussion groups are very easy to use. Once you master reading a topic, creating a topic, and replying to a topic, that's about it. You don't need to go through any registration procedure or use a particular browser to participate. The result is that there are no artificial barriers to participation, and everyone is encouraged to participate (so are spammers, but as you've already seen, FogBugz implements a defense-in-depth against spammers).

On the other hand, there are two features that are present in many discussion groups that FogBugz doesn't implement: e-mail notification and branching conversations. Both of these are deliberate omissions. If you allow people to subscribe to a conversation via e-mail (usually implemented with a checkbox that says something like "e-mail me if people reply to this post"), you've just removed the incentive people might have to come back to the discussion group. The result is that conversations will peter out quickly, and you'll have a hard (or impossible) time building any community. Eliminating this one little checkbox encourages (OK, forces) people to come back. While they're back, they might read a few more posts and contribute a few more of their own.

Branching conversations seem reasonable to programmers; let people reply to any post in a discussion and start a new thread of discussion from there. But if you implement branching, you'll find two things. First, it's incredibly hard to come up with a user interface that makes multiply branched conversations easy to follow. Second, the same idiots will branch every discussion in the same idiotic directions. Without branching, discussions tend to stay on a single track, which makes them much easier to follow.

Even such a simple decision as page arrangement can have major consequences. FogBugz, for example, always keeps topics sorted in the same order: the topic that was started most recently remains at the top of the list. Many other packages sort in order of most recent reply instead. With the FogBugz system, topics automatically age off the home page, rather than hanging around forever. This prevents perennial arguments from hijacking your forum, spawning discussions that run hundreds of replies, and scaring new users away.

Locating the Reply and New Topic links at the bottom of the lists is also a deliberate decision. This is a way to at least try to encourage people to read the discussion before replying. At the very least they have to scroll past it, and perhaps they'll notice that someone else has already made their point.

FogBugz doesn't show you the discussion thread while you're writing a reply. This is to encourage you to actually compose your own reply, rather than quoting what went before. Quoting may seem like a fine idea when you're writing a reply, but think about the next person to come along: do you really want to sentence them to read everything twice? I didn't think so.

A final note: none of these technical decisions will do the whole job of turning a discussion group into a useful, friendly, and energetic community. More and more companies these days are turning to having evangelists (or customer support representatives, or transparency managers, or whatever the heck they want to call them) whose job it is to promote community. If you're planning on using discussion groups as an important part of your public face, it's worth making sure that someone in your organization is passionate about community, and that they have promoting community as part of their official, paid job description.

Summary

In this chapter, you learned about two of the most important features of FogBugz: e-mail and discussion group management. You saw how you can use e-mail within your team, and as a means of communicating with customers, all under the control of FogBugz. You also learned how to set up and moderate discussion groups to help create a community around your products.

In the final chapter, I'll turn to one more major aspect of FogBugz, this one of great interest to software developers: integrating your bug reports and your source code control system.

CHAPTER 6

Working with
Source Code Control

FogBugz doesn't exist in isolation from the rest of your development processes. In particular, you can integrate FogBugz with a number of popular source code control systems:

- CVS

- Perforce

- Subversion

- Vault

- Visual SourceSafe

In this chapter, you'll learn how and why to work with source code control from within your FogBugz installation.

Understanding Source Code Control Integration

When you integrate FogBugz with a source code control system, you're setting up a two-way link between the two systems. This means two things:

- When you're looking at a case, you can see the code that was checked in to resolve the case.

- When you're looking at a code check-in, you can see the case that it was intended to fix.

These two-way links make it much easier to keep track of what's going on as your software makes its way from conception to release. Before showing you the actual mechanics of setting this stuff up, I'll go through a scenario in which the links come in very handy, and then discuss the different choices for source code control software to use with FogBugz.

Using Integration for Code Reviews

FogBugz's source code control integration makes it trivial for you to set up code reviews, which are an incredibly powerful tool for shipping high-quality software. The point of code reviews is to make sure that all source code gets checked for errors by another developer before it's checked into the master build. Some teams implement code reviews with a formal checklist of defects to watch out for. Others take a more informal approach, often having a senior developer read over code from junior developers. In any case, this technique has been proven to lead to higher-quality code *and* better developers, so it's certainly worth considering in your own organization.

With FogBugz integrated to a source code control system, a code review process might look like this:

1. Karen Benson, one of MegaUtilities' QA staff, is testing out the latest build of Service Monitor. She discovers that installing the software, uninstalling it, and then reinstalling it brings up the login information from the first installation: a potential security issue. She enters a bug, which FogBugz automatically assigns to the project lead, Valerie Shriver.

2. Valerie looks over the bug and decides that it's a setup issue. She assigns it to Paige Nagel, who's handling the installer coding.

3. Paige inspects the code and realizes that some registry keys aren't getting properly deleted on uninstall. She checks the appropriate source files out of the corporate source code control system and fixes the bug.

4. Paige checks the files back into the Development branch in the source code control system. When she does this, she includes a specially formatted comment with the case ID in her check-in comments. The source code control system notifies FogBugz of the check-in.

5. Paige assigns the bug back to Valerie, with a note that the fix is ready for code review.

6. Valerie opens the case. Because of the notification from the source code control system, FogBugz displays hyperlinks to the changed code right in the case itself. She clicks the links for the latest version of each file involved to see color-coded diffs, highlighting just the code that Paige changed. If Valerie needs more detail, she can drill into the entire history of any of the source files without leaving the FogBugz interface.

7. Satisfied with the code review, Valerie assigns the bug back to Paige with a note that the check-in is approved.

8. Paige marks the bug as resolved, and merges the changed code from the Development branch to the Release branch.

9. FogBugz assigns the bug back to Karen, who checks to make sure the fix is good and then marks the bug as closed.

Integration is also useful in the other direction, when you're working with source code control. Suppose you've just refreshed your local copy of a project with the latest shared source, and you can't figure out the point of a particular change in the code. Go to your source code control interface, locate the link back to FogBugz, and you can jump right to the case that was the reason for the change.

Choosing a Source Code Control System

With sufficient ingenuity, you can integrate nearly any source code control system with FogBugz. The minimum requirement is that you need to be able to run some sort of script on every check-in that either does a GET from a specially formatted URL or uses ODBC or OLE DB to insert records into a table. Fog Creek supports five source code control systems in particular. Each has its own pros and cons. Here's some information to help you choose the right one for your own purposes:

- CVS (https://www.cvshome.org/) is an open source project that has been around for quite a while and that has been proven on many applications. You can install a CVS server on many platforms, including Linux, Solaris, and Windows. It's free, and an excellent choice for many projects. Because it's been around for so long, there are many add-on tools available for CVS.

- Perforce (http://www.perforce.com/) runs on practically any modern platform, and has the widest support for graphical clients on various platforms of any source code control system I've seen. It has a particularly well-designed branching model that makes it suitable for complex projects. Perforce is free for up to two users, but starts at $750 per user after that.

- Subversion (http://subversion.tigris.org/) is meant to be a "better CVS." Like CVS, it's an open source project. In particular, some of the underlying operations are faster and more flexible than the CVS equivalents. Subversion isn't as mature as CVS, but it's also a good choice as a free system.

- Vault (http://www.sourcegear.com/vault/index.html) uses Microsoft SQL Server as a data repository for reliability, and it works very well over slow connections. It's also designed to be a painless upgrade for users who are familiar with Visual SourceSafe. It's the only one of these applications that offers built-in support for FogBugz integration. However, in addition to SQL Server licenses, you'll also need to pay $199 per user after the first user.

- Visual SourceSafe (http://msdn.microsoft.com/vstudio/previous/ssafe/) is Microsoft's source code control system. It comes with Visual Studio, and it's a good choice for developers who work exclusively within Visual Studio. But it has a reputation for being slow over WAN connections, and it has had data corruption problems in the past (both of these problems are supposed to be fixed in Visual SourceSafe 2005).

Making the Connection

You can set up source code integration between FogBugz and your source code control system in two steps. First, install a "trigger" script in your source control system to notify FogBugz whenever a check-in occurs that is related to a particular bug. The easiest way to notify FogBugz is to use an HTTP library to GET a URL of the following form, where bugID is the bug ID number, file is the file that is being checked in, x is the old revision number, and y is the new revision number:

```
http://fogbugzURL/cvsSubmit.asp?ixBug=bugID&sFile=file&sPrev=x&sNew=y
```

Alternatively, you can notify FogBugz by inserting records directly into the database table that it monitors for source code control communications. The table is named CVS, and it includes these columns:

- ixBug, the integer bug ID

- sFile, the 255-character-string name of the file

- sPrev, the 255-character-string old revision number

- sNew, the 255-character-string new revision number

■**Note** The revision numbers in this table are strings instead of integers because some source code control products let you assign arbitrary nonnumeric revision numbers when you check in code.

The second step in setting up integration is to configure FogBugz to create hyperlinks from the check-in information to a Web page showing the check-in logs or diffs. The URLs you'll need to use depend on the particular source code control system that you're employing, but all of the systems offer some Web interface that you can use, either built in or as an add-on.

In the remainder of this section, I'll give you more detailed instructions for setting up each of the supported source code control systems.

Setting Up CVS Integration

FogBugz comes with two integration scripts for CVS: one written in Perl, and one written in VBScript. If your CVS server runs on a Linux or Unix machine, you'll probably want to use the Perl version. If your CVS server runs on a Windows machine, you can install Perl and use the Perl script, but it's probably simpler to use the VBScript version. The installation instructions are similar either way. You'll find the scripts installed with FogBugz:

```
Program Files\FogBugz\Accessories\SourceControl\CVS\logBugData.pl
Program Files\FogBugz\Accessories\SourceControl\CVS\logBugData.vbs
```

Once you've located the appropriate script, follow these steps to set things up:

1. Open a command window on your CVS server and check out the CVSROOT directory by running this command:

   ```
   cvs co -d cvsroot  CVSROOT
   ```

2. Make the CVSROOT directory your current directory.

3. Create a file named bugz.txt in this directory. The file should contain a single line of text:

   ```
   CVS: BUGZID:
   ```

4. Save the file and add it to your CVS repository by running this command:

   ```
   cvs add bugz.txt
   ```

5. Copy the appropriate script file for your platform to the CVSHOME directory. If you're running on Unix, set execute permissions on this file.

6. Open the script file in a text editor. Near the top of the file, you'll find three settings that you need to customize:

   • Set the value of $BUGZ_SERVER to the DNS name of the Web server where FogBugz is running.

   • Set the value of $BUGZ_URL to the virtual path of your FogBugz installation. Normally this is /FogBugz/.

   • Set the value of $CVSSUBMIT to cvsSubmit.asp or cvsSubmit.php, depending on whether you're using the ASP or PHP version of FogBugz.

7. Save the script file and use cvs add to add it to your repository.

8. Edit the file rcsinfo to add one line of text to the end. If you're running on a Unix server, the line to add is

   ```
   ALL $CVSROOT/path/to/bugz.txt
   ```

   If you're running on a Windows server, use

   ```
   ALL $CVSROOT\path\to\bugz.txt
   ```

9. Edit the file loginfo to add one line of text to the end. If you're running on a Unix server, the line to add is

   ```
   ALL perl -s /path/to/cvs/logBugData.pl "%{sVv}"
   ```

   On Windows, use this line:

   ```
   ALL cscript.exe C:\path\to\logBugData.vbs "%{sVv}"
   ```

10. Edit the file checkoutlist, adding two lines at the end:

    ```
    bugz.txt Error-bugz.txt
    logBugData.pl Error-logBugData.pl
    ```

11. Check in your changes by running

    ```
    cvs commit
    ```

■**Tip** Each user will have to recheck out the source tree they are working on so that the CVS: BUGZID: line is added to the template for log notes. (Otherwise everything will still work, but they will have to remember to add BUGZID: manually each time they commit a change.)

Now it's time to set up the other end of the equation, letting FogBugz retrieve information from CVS:

1. Download and install the CVSweb project from http://www.freebsd.org/projects/ cvsweb.html to implement a Web interface to your CVS repository.

2. Log in to FogBugz as an administrator. Click the Site hyperlink on the Administrative Tools bar. Scroll down to find the Source Code Control URL settings shown in Figure 6-1.

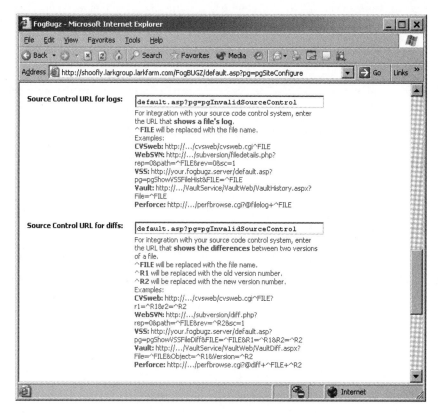

Figure 6-1. *Setting up source code control URLs in FogBugz*

3. Follow the instructions on screen to set up the proper URLs for calling CVSweb.

4. Click OK to save your settings.

Setting Up Perforce Integration

Like CVS, Perforce runs on a variety of servers. Thus, FogBugz supplies both Perl and VBScript integration scripts for Perforce as well:

```
Program Files\FogBugz\Accessories\SourceControl\Perforce\logBugDataP4.pl
Program Files\FogBugz\Accessories\SourceControl\Perforce\logBugDataP4.vbs
```

Follow these directions to set up FogBugz integration with Perforce:

1. Copy the appropriate script file into the Perforce installation directory.

2. Edit the script file, customizing it for your own FogBugz installation:

   • Set the value of $BUGZ_SERVER to the DNS name of the Web server running FogBugz, for example, www.example.com.

   • Set the value of $BUGZ_URL to the virtual path of your FogBugz installation. Normally this is /FogBugz/.

   • If you're using Perfoce passwords, add code at the end of the customization section. For Perl, add these lines of code:

   ```
   $UserName = $ARGV[3];
   $Password =  $ARGV[4];
   $ClientHost = $ARGV[5];
   $p4 = "p4 -p $ServerPort -c $ClientName -u $UserName -p $Password";
   ```

   • If you're using the VBScript integration script, add these lines instead:

   ```
   Dim UserName: UserName = args(3)
   Dim PassWord: PassWord = args(4)
   Dim ClientHost: ClientHost = args(5)
   Dim p4: p4 = "p4 -p " & ServerPort & " -c " & ClientName & _
     " -u  " & UserName &  " -p " & Password"
   ```

3. Add a trigger by typing **p4 triggers** at the command prompt. A text file appears. (If it doesn't, make sure p4, the Perforce executable, is in your path.) Add a line to the end of this file. (Note: if you have Perforce passwords enabled, add %password% after %user% in the trigger.) For the Perl version, the line to add is

   ```
   exTest //… "c::/perl/bin/perl.exe c:/path/logBugDataP4.pl %changelist%
   %serverport% %client% %user% %clienthost%"
   ```

   For the VBscript version, use this line instead:

   ```
   exTest //… "cscript.exe c:/path/logBugDataP4.vbs %changelist%
   %serverport% %client% %user% %clienthost%"
   ```

   Make sure to enter this code on a single line in the file, and to precede it with a single tab character.

4. Save the file to create the appropriate trigger.

To set up integration in the reverse direction so that FogBugz can display code from your Perforce repository, follow these steps:

1. Download and install the perfbrowse project from http://www.perforce.com/perforce/loadsupp.html to implement a Web interface to your Perforce repository.

2. Log in to FogBugz as an administrator. Click the Site hyperlink on the administration toolbar. Scroll down to find the Source Code Control URL settings.

3. Follow the instructions on screen to set up the proper URLs for calling perfbrowse.

4. Click OK to save your settings.

Setting Up Subversion Integration

Setting up Subversion integration is relatively simple, but you'll need to locate two files before you start. First, you need the actual integration script. You have your choice of Perl or VBScript versions:

```
Program Files\FogBugz\Accessories\SourceControl\Subversion\logBugDataSVN.pl
Program Files\FogBugz\Accessories\SourceControl\Subversion\logBugDataSVN.vbs
```

You'll also need the SubVersion-to-FogBugz post-commit hook file:

```
Program Files\FogBugz\Accessories\SourceControl\Subversion\post-commit.bat
```

Then follow these directions to set up the integration:

1. Put both files into the Hooks directory in your Subversion repository.

2. If your repository is on Unix, make sure to set execute permissions on your logBugDataSVN file.

3. Customize the script file as follows:

   • Set the value of $BUGZ_SERVER to the DNS name of the Web server where FogBugz is running.

   • Set the value of $BUGZ_URL to the virtual path of your FogBugz installation. Normally this is /FogBugz/.

   • Set the value of $CVSSUBMIT to cvsSubmit.asp or cvsSubmit.php, depending on whether you're using the ASP or PHP version of FogBugz.

4. Edit the post-commit.bat file and change the following line to point to your Subversion repository Hooks folder (and change .vbs to .pl if you're using the Perl version):

   ```
   C:\SubVersion\Repos\Hooks\logBugDataSVN.vbs
   ```

To set up integration in the reverse direction, so that FogBugz can display code from your Subversion repository, follow these steps:

1. Download and install the WebSVN project from http://websvn.tigris.org/ to implement a Web interface to your Subversion repository.

2. Log in to FogBugz as an administrator. Click the Site hyperlink on the Administrative Tools bar. Scroll down to find the Source Code Control URL settings.

3. Follow the instructions on screen to set up the proper URLs for calling WebSVN.

4. Click OK to save your settings.

Setting Up Vault Integration

Vault is unique among the supported source code control applications because the Vault developers have built FogBugz support directly into their side of the equation. To set up integration from the Vault side, run the Vault admin tool. Go to the Repository options and enter the main URL of your FogBugz server in the Bug Tracking Integration URL textbox, as shown in Figure 6-2. Click Apply to save the change.

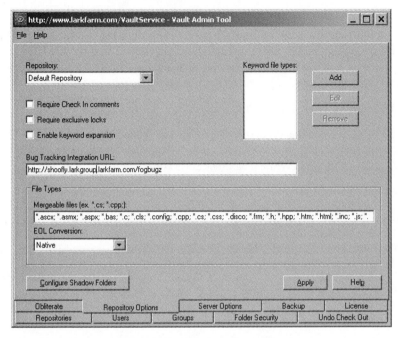

Figure 6-2. *Setting up Vault for FogBugz integration*

■**Note**: You can have different FogBugz URLs for different Vault repositories, or you can set an overall URL to be used by all repositories.

Setting up integration from the other side is equally simple, because there's no additional software to install:

1. Log in to FogBugz as an administrator. Click the Site hyperlink on the Administrative Tools bar. Scroll down to find the Source Code Control URL settings.

2. Follow the instructions on screen to set up the proper URLs for calling Vault.

3. Click OK to save your settings.

Setting Up Visual SourceSafe Integration

Visual SourceSafe doesn't support running triggers for every check-in. Fortunately, there's a trick you can use to get information about check-ins to Vault anyhow. You can tell Visual SourceSafe to keep a journal file, and then use a scheduled task to extract information from this file. Here's how to set this up:

1. Run the Visual SourceSafe 6.0 Admin program. Select Options from the Tools menu. On the General tab, enter the name of a file that Visual SourceSafe should use as a journal file. Click OK to save your change, and close the Admin program.

2. Install Visual SourceSafe to the FogBugz server machine. You must make sure that the FogBugz user or whoever you installed FogBugz to run as has read access on all your VSS folders and all subfolders. The user must also have full control on the names.dat and the rights.dat files, and the LoggedIn directory. Also, the user must have full control on the files SSUS.DLL and SSAPI.DLL in order to create the SourceSafe COM object.

3. Edit the vss_fbupdate.wsf file in the FogBugz\Accessories\SourceControl\VSS folder:

   • Edit the FB_PATH variable so that the script will pick up the needed info from the registry. (Note that you will have to add VSSUser and VSSPassword keys to the registry at HKEY_LOCAL_MACHINE\SOFTWARE\Fog Creek Software\FogBugz\[%FB_PATH%].)

   • Alternatively, you can override what is in the registry and manually set the sDBConnection to the connection string for FogBugz, and the FB_VSS_USER and FB_VSS_PASSWORD variables.

   • For each VSS project you have, add a line to the script beneath the commented-out line

   ```
   'Call ProcessVSSJournal("Project Name", "Path to VSS Database directory")
   ```

   For example (enter this as a single line in the file):

   ```
   Call ProcessVSSJournal("Test", "
   C:\program files\microsoft visual studio\common\vss")
   ```

▓**Note** If you are using MySQL for your FogBugz database, you cannot have an underscore in the file path, since it will be replaced by MySQL with a dash, and you cannot use a backslash, since MySQL will interpret that as an escape character. The solution is to use forward slashes in the filename instead.

---

4. Set the vss_fbupdate.wsf file to run as a scheduled task every so often (maybe hourly or even more often if you like). The task will complete very quickly, so do not worry about this script running too often. Make sure this task runs as a user that has privileges to rename and delete files in the VSS directories (usually not the FogBugz user, but instead an admin on the machine). Use the //B option to wscript so the script does NOT run in interactive mode. For example, you might use this command (entered as a single line at the command prompt):

   ```
   c:\winnt\system32\wscript.exe //B
   \progra~1\fogbugz\accessories\vss_fbupdate.wsf
   ```

Setting up integration from the FogBugz side is simple, because FogBugz includes special code to deal with Visual SourceSafe repositories:

1. Log in to FogBugz as an administrator. Click the Site hyperlink on the Administrative Tools bar. Scroll down to find the Source Code Control URL settings.

2. Follow the instructions on screen to set up the proper URLs for calling Visual SourceSafe.

3. Click OK to save your settings.

Getting from Cases to Code and Vice Versa

The key to making sure that everything works together is that when you're checking in code to your source control system, you need to tell FogBugz which case this code is meant to address. How you do this depends on the source code control system. If you're using CVS, Perforce, Subversion, or Visual SourceSafe, you need to include a specially formatted line in your check-in comments. For example, if you're checking in code for case 2587, you need to include (on a line by itself)

```
BugzID: 2587
```

If you're using Vault, the procedure is a bit different. Because Vault includes deep FogBugz integration, there's a spot right on the user interface for including the FogBugz case number. Figure 6-3 shows the Vault Commit dialog box. You can fill in a FogBugz case number in the Update Bugs textbox to have the code automatically linked to that case.

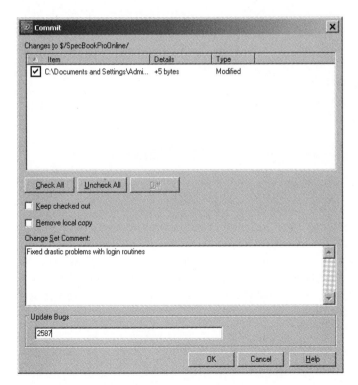

Figure 6-3. *Committing code in Vault with a FogBugz link*

What does it look like in action? Bearing in mind that the details of the Web interface change from program to program, I'll demonstrate with a simple bug. Figure 6-4 shows the original FogBugz bug report, which calls for a couple of easy user interface changes.

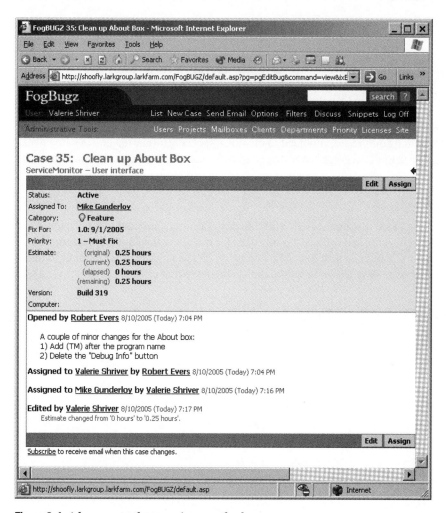

Figure 6-4. *A bug report that requires a code change*

After inspecting the bug report, I check out the appropriate files to make the changes. At this point, FogBugz isn't involved, except to tell me what needs to be done. So I make the necessary changes in the source code and make sure the project still passes my own unit tests. Satisfied, I check in the files to my Vault server, making sure to note the bug number on the check-in.

Figure 6-5 shows the tester's view of the bug at this point. You'll see that in addition to the usual FogBugz information, FogBugz has added a number of hyperlinks in the Checkins area.

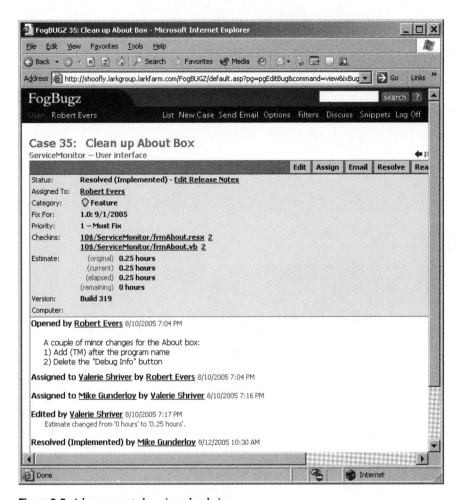

Figure 6-5. *A bug report showing check-ins*

Each file has two links. The first will take you to a screen containing the history of the file. Figure 6-6 shows this screen for a file in a Vault server. Hyperlinks let you see any version of the file, see its diff from the previous version, or tell who checked the changes in.

The other link displayed with each file takes you directly to a listing of the file, together with a diff from the previous version. Figure 6-7 shows a small portion of such a diff, which is color-coded to show lines that were added, deleted, or changed.

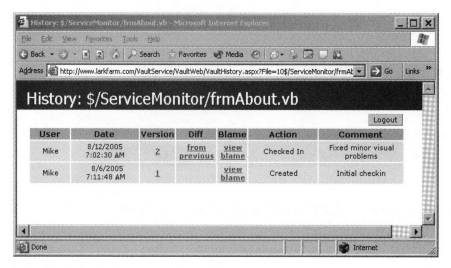

Figure 6-6. *File history shown in FogBugz*

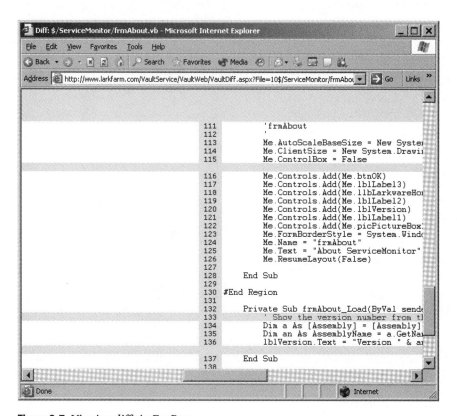

Figure 6-7. *Viewing diffs in FogBugz*

Summary

In this chapter, you learned about the integration between FogBugz and various source code control applications. You saw how to set up the integration and were introduced to some scenarios where it's very helpful to have this in place. With that, you know almost all of the ins and outs of FogBugz: you've gone from simply entering cases, through managing and administering the system, to using it in conjunction with your other programming tools.

There's one final key point to remember, though. Because FogBugz is supplied as ASP or PHP pages as well as an unlocked database, its source code is completely open. Though Fog Creek doesn't officially support users modifying their own installations, there's nothing to prevent you from making changes if you find something that doesn't quite work the way you'd like. I urge you to learn the system inside and out before you start tweaking, though. But if you do need to stretch the boundaries of FogBugz, open the pages in your favorite editor and you may find that the changes you need are easy to make.

APPENDIX A

■ ■ ■

Setting Up FogBugz

The FogBugz help file contains complete instructions on installing FogBugz. But there's a chicken-and-egg problem there: to see the help file, you need to install FogBugz. If you want to read the installation instructions before installing, you can find them on the Fog Creek Web site:

- Instructions for Windows:
  http://www.fogcreek.com/FogBugz/docs/40/Articles/Installing/Windows.html

- Instructions for Unix:
  http://www.fogcreek.com/FogBugz/docs/40/Articles/Installing/Unix.html

- Instructions for Macintosh:
  http://www.fogcreek.com/FogBugz/docs/40/Articles/Installing/MacOSX.html

But just in case your corporate policies prohibit reading Web pages from your server, or you just find having instructions on paper comforting, I'll review the instructions here. The server portion of FogBugz runs on Windows, Unix, or Macintosh servers; refer to the appropriate section of this appendix for your operating system.

Installing on Windows

If you're working with a Windows server, the most complex part of installing FogBugz is checking the system requirements. After that, installing the software itself is pretty simple.

Checking System Requirements for Windows

You probably won't have to worry about hardware for a FogBugz server. Any Pentium-class computer will probably be fine for most teams. At Fog Creek, they've run databases with over 100 users off of a single Pentium II/266 MHz. You'll probably want at least 512MB of RAM to get decent performance out of any Windows server.

FogBugz for Windows is supported on the following operating systems:

- Windows XP Professional

- Windows 2000 (Professional, Server, Advanced Server, or Datacenter)

- Windows Server 2003 (Web, Standard, Enterprise, or Datacenter)

FogBugz is compatible with Windows XP Professional Edition but not Home Edition. On Windows XP, you need to install Internet Information Services (IIS), which is not installed by default. If it is not installed, you can install it from Start ➤ Control Panel ➤ Add or Remove Programs ➤ Add or Remove Windows Components.

On Windows Server 2003, you should use the Manage Your Server application to install IIS. Click Add or Remove a Role and ensure that the Application Server role is turned on.

FogBugz also requires VBScript 5.6 or later and Microsoft Data Access Components (MDAC) 2.6 or later on the server. You can download VBScript from http://msdn.microsoft.com/library/default.asp?url=/downloads/list/webdev.asp. To find the latest version of MDAC, go to http://www.microsoft.com and enter MDAC in the search box.

You also need to have a database server installed. You have three choices for a database for FogBugz on Windows:

- Microsoft Jet 4.0SP3

- MySQL 4.0 or later

- Microsoft SQL Server 7.0 or 2000. At the time of this writing, SQL Server 2005 ("Yukon") was not yet available in final form from Microsoft, but Fog Creek assures me that they will support SQL Server 2005 shortly after it is released.

Microsoft Jet is preinstalled on Windows 2000 and later, so you probably don't have to install Jet. You can also install Jet for free from Microsoft's Web site; go to http://www.microsoft.com and enter "Jet" in the search box. Jet is good enough for small teams using FogBugz. It works fine for up to about 10 users. The major drawback to Jet as a FogBugz database is that it does not support full-text search.

MySQL is an extremely popular open source database available for free from MySQL AB. MySQL supports full-text search. You can download and install MySQL from http://www.mysql.com/.

Microsoft SQL Server is a commercial, industrial-strength database that will scale to virtually any size software team. It requires a license from Microsoft and makes FogBugz work faster and more reliably on larger teams. SQL Server supports full-text search.

If you've already got SQL Server installed on your network (or can afford to buy SQL Server licenses just for bug tracking), use SQL Server. For very small teams or casual bug tracking, use Jet. Otherwise, use MySQL.

To send e-mail, you need an SMTP server. If you have the ability to send Internet e-mail, you probably already have one of these somewhere. There is also a free SMTP server included in IIS. For FogBugz to receive incoming mail, you need a POP3 server. FogBugz supports plain POP3 and secure (ssh-based) POP3. Virtually all e-mail servers support POP3. Windows Server 2003 includes a built-in POP3 server.

Running Setup on Windows

Setting up FogBugz on a Windows server is as easy as double-clicking the FogBugz setup file and following the instructions on screen. FogBugz 4.0 setup uses a wizard interface to walk you through the setup one step at a time. At any point before you click Finish, you can cancel, and setup will roll back any changes you have already made.

FogBugz setup is designed to be as safe as possible. If anything goes wrong during the main phase (in which you see a progress indicator), after the error message is displayed, FogBugz setup gives up and rolls backwards. There are command-line arguments to the setup EXE program that can be used to ignore errors and continue anyway. To use these options, you need to launch setup from a command window, instead of by double-clicking the file:

- /ignoreiiserror will allow setup to continue even if it can't set up a virtual directory in IIS. You will need to create a virtual directory manually and map it to the FogBugz website directory.

- /ignorepermissionserror will allow setup to continue even if it can't set permissions for the FogBugz account (that you specify during setup) to access the FogBugz directory. You will need to grant full permission for the FogBugz account to access the FogBugz directory manually.

- /sqlserveronly will tell setup to install only the SQL Server components. This is useful if your SQL Server machine is a different machine from your IIS machine and they are not on the same domain.

■Note Setup never requires a reboot. While files are being copied, it temporarily stops three services: W3SVC (the Web service), CISVC (the Content Indexing Service), and FogBugz's own Dispatcho or Maintenance service (during an upgrade).

Installing on Unix

If you're setting up FogBugz on Unix, you need to spend some time making sure that various software prerequisites are installed. After that, installing FogBugz itself is a matter of extracting files and running a setup script.

Checking System Requirements for Unix

FogBugz for Unix runs on 100% Intel-compatible computers (386, 486, Pentium, etc.). Other CPUs will not work. FogBugz has been tested with and is supported on these operating systems:

- Red Hat Linux 8.0

- Red Hat Linux 9.0

- Mandrake Linux 9.2

- SuSE Linux 9.0

- Debian Linux 3.0r1

- FreeBSD 5.1

Other versions of Linux that are binary compatible with these may work, but they are not officially supported.

> **▓Tip** If you're not sure which version of Unix you have, type **uname -a** at the command prompt.

The Apache HTTP server must be installed and running. You'll need version 1.3 or 2.0 to run FogBugz. The easiest way to tell if Apache is running on your server is to point a Web browser at it. For example, from the command line, type **lynx http://localhost**. If Apache is running, the command **apachectl status** will usually tell you what version you have. Or you can try to download a page that doesn't exist, which will display an error message containing the version of Apache. For example, type **lynx http://localhost/xxxx**.

You'll also need the PHP command-line interpreter, version 4.2.2 or later (but not PHP 5.0, which is not supported), which you can download from http://ca2.php.net/manual/en/features.commandline.php. This is a version of the PHP scripting language that runs from the command line. The xml, imap, and mysql extensions must be compiled in PHP.

> **▓Tip** If you're not sure whether PHP is installed, the command php -v will try to run it and tell you what version you have. The command php -m will show you which extensions you have installed. On some systems, php may be named php4. In this case, you can make a symbolic link from php to php4.

You also need to have pear in your path or in /usr/local/php/bin/pear. Type **which pear** to find out whether your path includes the pear binary.

You'll need to have the PHP scripting language (http://www.php.net) installed as well. Yes, this is different from the PHP command-line interpreter. PHP must have the xml, imap, and mysql extensions compiled, and the version must be at least 4.2.2, but not 5.0 or later.

> **▓Caution** Although FogBugz will run on PHP 4.2.2, I recommend you get the latest version of PHP 4 (4.3.10 as of this writing). There are important security fixes in recent versions.

To check whether PHP is installed, create a file named test.php in a directory that is served by your Web server. Copy the following text into that file:

```
<?
echo PHP_VERSION . "<br>";
echo "XML:" . extension_loaded('xml') . "<br>";
echo "imap:" . extension_loaded('imap') . "<br>";
echo "mysql:" . extension_loaded('mysql') . "<br>";
?>
```

Now browse to that new page with a Web browser, for example, **lynx http://localhost/test.php**. If you see either the PHP source code itself or your Web browser offers to download the file to you, this means your HTTP server is not configured to run PHP files. See the PHP documentation for instructions on configuring Apache to run PHP files.

If PHP is running, you will see the PHP version in the first line. Check that it is 4.2.2 or later.

The next three lines tell you whether PHP was compiled with xml, imap, and mysql support, respectively. If they are, you will see the number 1 after the colon. For example:

```
4.3.3
XML:1
imap:1
mysql:1
```

On Unix, you need to use MySQL, version 4.0 or later, to host the FogBugz database. You can download MySQL from http://www.mysql.com. To check whether MySQL is running, type **mysql** at the command line:

- If you get "Command not found," you probably don't have MySQL installed, or it might not be in your path.

- If you get "Can't connect to local MySQL server," it's possible you only have the client installed, or it could be that the server (mysqld) is simply not running.

- If you get "Welcome to the MySQL monitor," you're probably in good shape. It should also tell you what version you're running.

Finally, your Unix server needs to be running the curl command-line tool from http://curx.haxx.se. Type **curl --version** at the command line. If curl is installed, you will see a version number. If you get the message "Command not found," install curl.

Setting Up FogBugz on Unix

To install FogBugz, log on as root or issue the su command. Before you start, you'll need to know three things about your system. Figure these out and make a note of them:

- The group under which Apache runs

- The location of your Apache Web server configuration file

- The location of your php.ini configuration file

FogBugz is delivered as a .tar.gz file. Uncompress this file in the directory where you want FogBugz to live. Fog Creek recommends /opt:

```
$ mv FogBugz-setup-php-*.tar.gz /opt
$ cd /opt
$ tar zxf FogBugz-setup-php-*.tar.gz
$ cd FogBugz
```

Now run the install.php script:

```
$ php -d output_buffering=0 -f install.php
```

Note The buffering setting is the number zero, not the letter O.

After the script file completes its work, launch your Web browser and navigate to http://localhost/FogBugz/install1.php to finish installing FogBugz. Now you need to set up the FogBugz Maintenance Service daemon, fpgbugzd. To start the daemon manually, enter these commands:

```
$ cd (your FogBugz directory)
$ cd Accessories
$ ./dispatchod start
```

You'll probably also want to add the daemon to your server's startup script so that it starts automatically. How you do this depends on which variety of Unix you're using:

Red Hat or Mandrake Linux Add this line to the bottom of your /etc/rc.local file:

```
(your FogBugz directory)/Accessories/fogbugzd start
```

Debian Linux Create this shell script in your /etc/rc.boot directory, named fogbugzd.sh:

```
#!/bin/sh
(your FogBugz directory)/Accessories/fogbugzd start
```

Make the script executable:

```
$ chmod +x fogbugzd.sh
```

SuSE Linux Add this line to the bottom of your /etc/init.d/boot.local file:

```
(your FogBugz directory)/Accessories/fogbugzd start
```

FreeBSD Create this shell script in your /usr/local/etc/rc.d directory, named fogbugzd.sh:

```
#!/bin/sh
(your FogBugz directory)/Accessories/fogbugzd start
```

Make the script executable:

```
$ chmod +x fogbugzd.sh
```

Installing on Macintosh

If you're setting up FogBugz on a Macintosh server, you need to spend some time making sure that various software prerequisites are installed. After that, installing FogBugz itself is a matter of running a setup program.

Checking System Requirements for a Macintosh Server

FogBugz for Macintosh runs on PowerPC Apple Macintosh computers running Mac OS X version 10.3 (Panther) or version 10.2.4 (Jaguar). Other systems will not work.

The Apache HTTP server must be installed and running. You'll need version 1.3 or 2.0 to run FogBugz. To check whether Apache is installed, launch System Preferences, and click Sharing. There should be a check mark next to "Personal Web Server." Alternatively, you can just point a browser at your own server. For example, try loading http://localhost in Safari or Internet Explorer. To check the version of Apache, try to download a page that doesn't exist, which will display an error message containing the version of Apache. For example, type **lynx http://localhost/xxxx**.

You'll also need the PHP command-line interpreter, version 4.2.2 or later (but not PHP 5.0, which is not supported), which you can download from http://ca2.php.net/manual/en/features.commandline.php. This is a version of the PHP scripting language that runs from the command line. The xml, imap, and mysql extensions must be compiled in PHP.

■Tip If you're not sure whether PHP is installed, the command php -v will try to run it and tell you what version you have. The command php -m will show you which extensions you have installed. On some systems, php may be named php4. In this case, you can make a symbolic link from php to php4.

You also need to have pear in your path or in /usr/local/php/bin/pear. Type **which pear** to find out whether your path includes the pear binary.

You'll need to have the PHP scripting language (http://www.php.net) installed as well. Yes, this is different from the PHP command-line interpreter. PHP must have the xml, imap, and mysql extensions compiled, and the version must be at least 4.2.2, but not 5.0 or later.

■Caution Although FogBugz will run on PHP 4.2.2, I recommend you get the latest version of PHP 4 (4.3.10 as of this writing). There are important security fixes in recent versions.

To check whether PHP is installed, create a file named test.php in a directory that is served by your Web server. Copy the following text into that file:

```
<?
echo PHP_VERSION . "<br>";
echo "XML:" . extension_loaded('xml') . "<br>";
echo "imap:" . extension_loaded('imap') . "<br>";
echo "mysql:" . extension_loaded('mysql') . "<br>";
?>
```

Now browse that new page with a Web browser, for example, **lynx http://localhost/test.php**. If you see either the PHP source code itself or your Web browser offers to download the file to you, this means your HTTP server is not configured to run PHP files. See the PHP documentation for instructions on configuring Apache to run PHP files.

If PHP is running, you will see the PHP version in the first line. Check that it is 4.2.2 or later.

The next three lines tell you whether PHP was compiled with xml, imap, and mysql support, respectively. If they are, you will see the number 1 after the colon. For example:

```
4.3.3
XML:1
imap:1
mysql:1
```

On the Macintosh, you need to use MySQL, version 4.0 or later, to host the FogBugz database. You can download MySQL from http://www.mysql.com. To check whether MySQL is running, type **mysql** at the command line:

- If you get "Command not found," you probably don't have MySQL installed, or it might not be in your path.

- If you get "Can't connect to local MySQL server," it's possible you only have the client installed, or it could be that the server (mysqld) is simply not running.

- If you get "Welcome to the MySQL monitor," you're probably in good shape. It should also tell you what version you're running.

■**Caution** The version of MySQL that comes with Mac OS X SERVER is broken. It yields incorrect results for SELECT COUNT queries. If you are running the default Mac OS X SERVER edition, you will need to reinstall MySQL from http://www.mysql.com. You can use the mysqldump command to back up your databases.

Finally, your Macintosh server needs to be running the curl command-line tool from http://curx.haxx.se. Type **curl --version** at the command line. If curl is installed, you will see a version number. If you get the message "Command not found," install curl.

Setting Up FogBugz on a Macintosh Server

To install FogBugz for Macintosh on an OS X server, double-click the .dmg file that you downloaded, and double-click the package inside that (it looks like a box). You will be guided through setup step by step. After the GUI-based setup is finished, it will launch your Web browser to let you finish configuring your system.

Understanding the FogBugz Maintenance Service

FogBugz does almost all its work through the Web, via a Web-based interface. That means that FogBugz code won't run until a user requests a Web page in their browser.

Typically, Web-based interfaces have two problems:

- Operations that take a long time make the user wait and result in a nonresponsive UI.

- Operations can only be initiated when a user hits a Web page. This makes it impossible to perform routine tasks such as deleting old spam at midnight or sending out the morning escalation report via e-mail.

To address these issues, FogBugz requires the FogBugz Maintenance Service (informally known as "the heartbeat") to be running at all times. This service's entire job is to wake up every few seconds and hit a Web page (specifically, heartbeat.asp). That Web page checks whether there's any maintenance work to be done, and, if there is, does it.

The FogBugz Maintenance Service is responsible for the following tasks:

- Receiving incoming e-mail via POP3

- Sending outgoing e-mail from the FogBugz outgoing mail queue (a table named MailQueue) using SMTP

- Performing the Bayesian learning algorithm after someone has reclassified an e-mail message or discussion group topic

- Deleting old spam messages permanently

- Sending the daily e-mail escalation report to any subscribers

If any of these tasks are not happening, it may be because the FogBugz Maintenance Service is not running. If the page heartbeat.asp has not been hit for a long time, FogBugz takes this as a sign that something is wrong with the FogBugz Maintenance Service and reports an error to the next administrator who logs on.

■Note The FogBugz Web interface will continue to function even if the FogBugz Maintenance Service is down, so users can continue to enter, work with, resolve, and close cases.

Customizing FogBugz

You learned in Chapter 3 how to customize FogBugz for your own development organization by creating projects, areas, clients, and so on. Maintaining these areas of FogBugz is likely to be an ongoing job for your FogBugz administrator. But there are other FogBugz options that you probably won't change often. As part of setting up FogBugz, the administrator should check and configure these settings. There's also a second configuration process to go through for individual users. FogBugz administrators can change these user options, or users can change their own options.

Site Configuration

To adjust the overall configuration of your FogBugz site, log in as an administrator and click the Site link on the Administrative Tools bar. You can change these settings on the Site Configuration screen:

- *SMTP Server*: Enter the network name, DNS name, or IP address of your outgoing mail server. Enter localhost if the mail server is on the same machine as FogBugz. Enter NONE if you don't want FogBugz to send any notification e-mail at all.

- *SMTP User*: If your SMTP server requires you to log in, provide the username here.

- *SMTP Password*: If your SMTP server requires you to log in, provide the password here.

- *Notification Return Address*: This is the apparent return address for notification e-mails. Usually, you want this to be a fake address, so people don't reply to those automatic mails. The example.com domain is reserved for fake addresses, so that's what FogBugz defaults to.

- *Log On Method*: FogBugz offers three log on methods with increasing levels of security. The first is "Names in dropdown, no passwords." This provides no security, and lets anyone log on to any account. This method is useful in small organizations where you trust everyone and are behind a firewall so there is no risk of public access to the FogBugz server. The second log on method is "Names in dropdown, with passwords." Every user can have a password, but the list of users is shown in a drop-down box in the log on screen. This will allow anyone who can access the FogBugz server to determine a list of names of users. If some of those users had blank or easily guessed passwords, a malicious user could break into FogBugz. The final method is "Type email address and password." This provides a moderate level of security, forcing each user to type their address and password to log on, and does not provide a public list of users.

- *Log on*: Determines whether the "Remember me at this computer" option appears on the log on page.

- *New User Control*: Normally only administrators can create FogBugz accounts. By changing this setting to "Anybody can create an account," you will allow anyone who can access FogBugz to make their own account. This is useful if your FogBugz server is secure inside a firewall and you have a large number of potential users in your organization.

- *Database*: These controls let you choose the type of database server and enter the connection string for the server. FogBugz will normally set this during setup.

- *Extra Fields*: Lets you set up any two text fields (such as Version and Computer) that will be included with cases.

- *FogBugz URL*: The full URL of the FogBugz server.

- *Working Schedule*: A hyperlink to the screen where you can adjust the working schedule (which is used for calculating due dates).

- *Source Control URL for Logs*: The URL to use for displaying source code control logs.

- *Source Control URL for Diffs*: The URL to use for displaying source code control diffs.

- *Date Format*: The format to use for displaying dates. The default is to query the user's browser for the setting to use.

- *Upload File Size Maximum*: The maximum size for a file that can be uploaded as an attachment to a case.

- *Reset FogBugz Autosort*: If you've made serious changes to the way that you want to classify incoming messages, you can click this link to tell FogBugz AutoSort to start its learning process over again.

■**Caution** The SMTP username and password will be stored in clear text in the Windows registry so that FogBugz can use them to log on whenever needed. Also note that SMTP is a clear-text protocol, so if the SMTP server is on a different computer, the username and password will be sent in clear text across the network.

User Options

The Options screen (available from the Options link in the main toolbar) lets you configure your personal options in FogBugz. Anyone who is logged on as an administrator can change the options for any user; everyone else can only change their own options.

You can configure the following:

- *Full Name*: Your full name as it appears in FogBugz.

- *Email Address*: The e-mail address that FogBugz will use to contact you. If you wish to receive multiple copies of each notification e-mail at different addresses, separate the addresses by commas.

- *Phone Number*: This will be displayed so that other users can contact you to ask questions without waiting for e-mail.

- *Escalation Report*: Check this box to receive a copy of the morning escalation report each day.

- *Snippet Activation Key*: The keystroke that you can use to insert a snippet into edit fields.

- *Display*: The information to be displayed in lists of cases.

You can also use the Options screen to change your password.

Adding Licenses

If business is going well, you'll probably need to add additional FogBugz licenses to accommodate more developers and testers. Fortunately, this is an easy process once you've purchased the licenses. When you purchase licenses, Fog Creek will e-mail you an order ID. To install the licenses, log on as an administrator. Click the Licenses link in the Administrative Tools bar. Enter the e-mail address and order ID from your purchase. Click the OK button, and your new licenses will be ready to use.

■**Note** If your FogBugz computer isn't connected to the public Internet, follow the link on the licenses page to an alternate data entry page where you can type in the license number and signature that Fog Creek will provide on request.

APPENDIX B

■ ■ ■

Using BugzScout

You've seen how easy it is to enter bug reports through the FogBugz interface. But wouldn't it be easier to not enter them at all? That's the reasoning behind BugzScout, a technology that works with FogBugz to programmatically submit bug reports. By incorporating BugzScout into your own applications, you can make it possible for those applications to submit bugs from the field. The only requirement is that the end user be able to see your FogBugz server via HTTP.

Installing BugzScout

After you've installed FogBugz on your server, open the accessories folder under your main FogBugz folder. In it you'll find a file named BugzScout.dll. Copy this to your development computer and register it using this command line:

```
regsvr32 bugzscout.dll
```

The BugzScout library contains a single object, BugzScoutCtl. Table B-1 shows the interface supported by this object.

Table B-1. *BugzScoutCtl Interface*

Member	Type	Description
Area	Property	Project area to contain this bug
DefaultMessage	Property	Default message to return to the user
Project	Property	Project to contain this bug
URL	Property	URL of your FogBugz server
UserName	Property	User to use when creating the bug
SubmitBug	Method	Sends the bug to the server
Failure	Event	Raised if the submission fails
Progress	Event	Raised while the submission is underway
Success	Event	Raised if the submission succeeds

Tip FogBugz includes the full source code for the BugzScout library. You'll find it in the ScoutSample.zip file in your accessories folder. Look for the BugzScoutCPP folder inside of the zip file.

Using BugzScout from Visual Basic

To use BugzScout from any ActiveX host, follow these steps:

1. Create an instance of the BugzScoutCtl object. Because BugzScout submits its bug reports asynchronously over HTTP, you must ensure that this object does not go out of scope before the success or failure events are posted.

2. Set the properties of the object to represent the bug that you want entered in the FogBugz database.

3. Call the SubmitBug method.

Here's an example of using BugzScout from a Visual Basic 6.0 application:

```
Option Explicit
' Declare the BugzScout object at the form level so
' that it will persist and we can trap its events
Dim WithEvents scout As BUGZSCOUTLib.BugzScoutCtl

' User email. We'd prompt for this during setup and
' store it somewhere.
Dim strUserEmail As String

Private Sub cmdMonitor_Click()
    On Error GoTo ErrHandler

    ' Do some actual work here

ExitHere:
    Exit Sub

ErrHandler:
    ' Call our bug-handling routine
    HandleError ("cmdMonitor_Click")
    Resume ExitHere

End Sub
```

```
Private Function HandleError(strCallingFunction As String)
    ' Generic handler for errors
    ' Submits the error-causing routine to FogBugz
    If scout Is Nothing Then
        Set scout = New BUGZSCOUTLib.BugzScoutCtl
        With scout
            .Project = "ServiceMonitor"
            .Area = "Misc"
            .URL = "http://shoofly.larkgroup.larkfarm.com/FogBugz/ScoutSubmit.asp"
            .UserName = "Robert Evers"
            .DefaultMessage = "The error has been sent to MegaUtilities"
        End With
    End If


    ' Submit the bug
    scout.SubmitBug "Error in " & strCallingFunction, "MainForm", _
     strUserEmail, False


End Function


Private Sub scout_Failure(ByVal sError As String)
    Debug.Print sError
End Sub

Private Sub scout_Success(ByVal sContents As String)
    Debug.Print sContents
End Sub
```

This code sample shows a generic function (HandleError) that you'd call from anywhere in your code. This function is responsible for initializing the BugzScoutCtrl object and setting its properties, then calling the SubmitBug method. SubmitBug takes four parameters:

- A string parameter that will be the title of the case created in FogBugz.

- A string parameter containing any extra information you care to pass. This parameter will be appended to the notes of the case.

- A string parameter that is the e-mail address of the person submitting the case. This will be used for the correspondent link on the case.

- A Boolean parameter that you can set to True to force the creation of a new case or False to allow this report to be appended to an otherwise identical existing case.

When the ScoutSubmit method finishes its work, the object will fire one of two events, Success or Failure. Success fires if the communication with the FogBugz server actually happens. It returns with a simple XML payload. It contains either an element called Success or one called Error, similar to these examples:

```
<?xml version="1.0"?>
<Success>Thank you for submitting your bug!</Success>
<?xml version="1.0"?>
<Error>No username found: George Swenson</Error>
```

The Success payload returns with either the DefaultMessage property provided when the bug was submitted, or a message added by someone on the bug server, such as "This bug has been fixed in version 2.0. Please upgrade." If you choose, you can show this to your users after the bug was submitted to give them an idea of why that bug happened or how to fix it. If there's an error after communicating with the server, the Error element contains the error message.

The Failure event fires if the communication with the server failed. For instance, this can happen because the URL field was not set correctly.

■**Note** BugzScout uses the ScoutSubmit Web page to enter its bugs into the database. Refer to Chapter 2 for more information on ScoutSubmit.

Using BugzScout from C#

You could use the BugzScout ActiveX object from a .NET language via COM Interop, but there's a better way. In the FogBugz accessories folder on your hard drive, you'll find the ScoutSample.zip file. The BugzScout.Net folder within this zip file contains two C# .NET projects:

- BugzScout is a complete C# implementation of BugzScout.

- ScoutSample is an example of calling the C# version of BugzScout.

Because .NET supports calling across languages, you can use the C# version of BugzScout from any .NET language. Its interface is quite similar to the ActiveX version. Table B-2 shows the members of the BugReport object in the C# version of BugzScout.

Table B-2. *BugReport Interface*

Member	Type	Description
Area	Property	Project area to contain this bug
DefaultMsg	Property	Default message to return to the user
Description	Property	Description of the bug
Email	Property	E-mail address of the bug submitter
ExtraInformation	Property	Additional information for the notes of the bug
FogBugzURL	Property	URL of your FogBugz server

Table B-2. *BugReport Interface (Continued)*

Member	Type	Description
FogBugzUserName	Property	User to use when creating the bug
ForceNewBug	Property	Set to true to force a new bug
Project	Property	Project to contain this bug
AppendAssemblyList	Method	Appends a list of assemblies and versions to the bug
Submit	Method	Sends the bug to the server

Here's a calling example from the ScoutSample project:

```
private void CustomReport(object sender, System.EventArgs e){
    try{
        BugReport bug = new BugReport(txtUrl.Text, txtUserName.Text);
        bug.Project = txtProject.Text;
        bug.Area = txtArea.Text;
        bug.Description = txtDescription.Text;
        bug.ExtraInformation = txtExtraInfo.Text;
        bug.ForceNewBug = chkForceNewBug.Checked;
        bug.Email = txtEmail.Text;
        bug.DefaultMsg = txtDefaultMessage.Text;
        lblStatus.Text = bug.Submit();
        lblStatus.ForeColor = Color.Green;
    }
    catch(Exception ex){
        lblStatus.ForeColor = Color.Red;
        lblStatus.Text = ex.Message;
    }
}
```

The .NET version of BugzScout uses a slightly different strategy from the ActiveX one for returning information. In case of success, the success message is returned as the return value from the Submit method. In case of any error, the BugReport class raises an exception.

Choosing What to Report

The most dangerous part of BugzScout is the ability to include extra information with the bug report. Developers are often tempted (probably through copying other applications) to capture everything they can think of: hardware and software configuration, time of day, speed of the user's Internet connection, the versions of every DLL on the system, and even complete memory dumps.

There are two good reasons why you should resist this temptation. First, users will find such full reporting to be an invasion of their privacy, which will make them less inclined to let your software automatically report bugs (and don't even *think* of reporting the bugs without asking for user permission, unless you want to be branded far and wide as a spyware vendor).

Second, most of the information will be worthless in most cases. As long as you have a way to get back to the user, knowing the line of code where the crash occurred is enough information to diagnose almost any problem.

Keeping the information you send back to a minimum has another benefit: it makes the HTTP communication process faster, which means that bug reporting is less intrusive to users. And that in turn makes them more likely to report bugs.

Here are a few other tips for making good use of BugzScout:

- Rather than assign all the bugs to a single person (who might move to another project or even leave the company while your application is still in use), assign them to a virtual account with a name such as "Bugs From the Field." Project managers can search through bugs assigned to this pseudo-person and assign the important ones to actual developers.

- FogBugz identifies duplicate bug reports through their titles, so consider putting information in the title to uniquely identify the bug. You might, for example, put the product name, line number, and error number in the title, and other information in the description.

- If it looks like the bug is in your error-handling code, be suspicious. There might be something so drastically wrong elsewhere that it's thoroughly scrambling the program's state.

- Look at automatic bug reports promptly, especially during beta periods. This gives you a chance to ask users for more information while the crash is still fresh in their minds.

INDEX

forums.apress.com
FOR PROFESSIONALS BY PROFESSIONALS™

JOIN THE APRESS FORUMS AND BE PART OF OUR COMMUNITY. You'll find discussions that cover topics of interest to IT professionals, programmers, and enthusiasts just like you. If you post a query to one of our forums, you can expect that some of the best minds in the business—especially Apress authors, who all write with *The Expert's Voice*™—will chime in to help you. Why not aim to become one of our most valuable participants (MVPs) and win cool stuff? Here's a sampling of what you'll find:

DATABASES
Data drives everything.

Share information, exchange ideas, and discuss any database programming or administration issues.

INTERNET TECHNOLOGIES AND NETWORKING
Try living without plumbing (and eventually IPv6).

Talk about networking topics including protocols, design, administration, wireless, wired, storage, backup, certifications, trends, and new technologies.

JAVA
We've come a long way from the old Oak tree.

Hang out and discuss Java in whatever flavor you choose: J2SE, J2EE, J2ME, Jakarta, and so on.

MAC OS X
All about the Zen of OS X.

OS X is both the present and the future for Mac apps. Make suggestions, offer up ideas, or boast about your new hardware.

OPEN SOURCE
Source code is good; understanding (open) source is better.

Discuss open source technologies and related topics such as PHP, MySQL, Linux, Perl, Apache, Python, and more.

PROGRAMMING/BUSINESS
Unfortunately, it is.

Talk about the Apress line of books that cover software methodology, best practices, and how programmers interact with the "suits."

WEB DEVELOPMENT/DESIGN
Ugly doesn't cut it anymore, and CGI is absurd.

Help is in sight for your site. Find design solutions for your projects and get ideas for building an interactive Web site.

SECURITY
Lots of bad guys out there—the good guys need help.

Discuss computer and network security issues here. Just don't let anyone else know the answers!

TECHNOLOGY IN ACTION
Cool things. Fun things.

It's after hours. It's time to play. Whether you're into LEGO® MINDSTORMS™ or turning an old PC into a DVR, this is where technology turns into fun.

WINDOWS
No defenestration here.

Ask questions about all aspects of Windows programming, get help on Microsoft technologies covered in Apress books, or provide feedback on any Apress Windows book.

HOW TO PARTICIPATE:
Go to the Apress Forums site at **http://forums.apress.com/**.
Click the New User link.